HARRY'S ROADHOUSE COOKBOOK

HARRY'S ROADHOUSE COOKBOOK

HARRY SHAPIRO AND PEYTON YOUNG

PHOTOGRAPHS BY JACK KOTZ

ILLUSTRATIONS BY JOEL NAKAMURA

Gibbs Smith, Publisher
Salt Lake City

First Edition
10 09 08 07 06   5 4 3 2 1

Published by
Gibbs Smith, Publisher
P.O. Box 667
Layton, Utah 84041

Orders: 1.800.748.5439
www.gibbs-smith.com

Designed by Maria Hwang Levy
Printed and bound in Hong Kong

Library of Congress Cataloging-in-Publication Data

Shapiro, Harry, 1947-
Harry's Roadhouse cookbook / Harry Shapiro and Peyton Young.— 1st ed.
p. cm.
Includes index.
ISBN 1-58685-838-6
1. Cookery, American. 2. Harry's Roadhouse (Restaurant : Santa Fe, N.M.)
I. Young, Peyton, 1965- II. Harry's Roadhouse (Restaurant : Santa Fe,
N.M.) III. Title.

TX715.S1473 2006
641.5973—dc22
2006000359

CONTENTS

FOREWORD 6

ACKNOWLEDGMENTS 9

INTRODUCTION 11

ROADHOUSE BASICS 16

DESSERTS 18

BREAKFAST 46

APPETIZERS 72

SALADS 84

SQUARE MEALS 100

SIDES 144

INDEX 156

FOREWORD

A few years ago when Harry's Roadhouse opened its doors after an extensive remodeling project, the cars started rolling in at dawn. Soon the gravel parking lot filled up with die-hard Harry's patrons who hadn't had their fix in two long months.

An impatient line formed outside and stretched around the building. You had to wait for over an hour to get a table. As breakfast slipped into brunch, and then lunch into dinner, the wait grew to two hours, then three. And still they kept coming.

Finally at ten at night on that big reopening day, co-owner Peyton Young stared out in disbelief at this madding crowd. There was no end in sight. She was exhausted and wanted to go home. But people kept pressing toward the hostess with desperate looks in their eyes, like crazed wildebeests in rut.

Finally, in a moment of understandable frustration, Peyton said to a friend (my wife, actually): "What is it with these people—why don't they just go home? Can't they . . . cook for themselves?"

No Peyton, we can't. Or at least we don't want to. We would rather wait in line for three hours for the Harry's signature meatloaf and a slice of your coconut cream pie.

It was on that long, busy day, I think, that Harry and Peyton fully realized they had created something more than a hit restaurant. What they had created was a need—an addiction, you might say. That's what great neighborhood restaurants are, really: habit-formers. In a given week, Harry's may serve upwards of five thousand people, but what's remarkable is that more than seventy-five percent of those people are locals who keep coming back for more and more and more—the Harry's addicts.

This fact is all the more remarkable when one remembers that Santa Fe is a tourist city world famous for its cuisine. It's a restaurant town, crawling with great chefs and people who know good food. But even in a culinary capital—especially in a culinary capital—there needs to be a place where the locals eat.

In Santa Fe, that place is Harry's.

The waits have gotten more manageable since that fateful reopening day, but the crowds never really faded. Drive by Harry's most any hour and you'll still see a used car lot—mud-spattered pickups with horse trailers and sleek Porsches and tofu-burning hippie vans and big honkin' Humvees—an absolute embarrassment of vehicles spilling out onto the road. All these years later, these people still won't cook for themselves.

Which begs the question: Why won't they? Why is Harry's so popular? It's a question that many of us around here, even die-hard fans like me, ask in a navel-gazing sort of way—a local puzzlement. We ask it in the way that Montanans might wonder why the big trout seem to congregate in a certain enigmatic hole in the river. Or in the way Irishmen in Doolin or Galway might hunker with their pints of Guinness and appreciatively parse the charms of a certain traditional folksinger. Isn't this something? What accounts for this little mystery?

It's the location, people often say about Harry's. Or it's the atmosphere. Or the good if slightly irascible waiters, who will, on occasion, call you "hon." Or the dearth of other mid-priced establishments in this bodaciously expensive town.

In truth, it's probably a little bit of all those things. But my answer to the mystery is much simpler. Why is Harry's so popular? It's the food!

The food at Harry's is consistently exceptional. It's inventive and at the same time familiar. The menu is sophisticated without succumbing to pretense, each item offered with a fresh, understated ambition. One dish may be aggressively regional and even redneck in its American sensibilities (Cajun Jambalaya or Pennsylvania-Dutch

Scrapple) and then the next dish will slay you with its cosmopolitan zest (a Kahlua flan or a Moroccan tagine). Truly, Harry's is all over the culinary map: brisket, lobster, curry, migas, Asian noodles, pot pies, po'boys. They serve a mean Seared Ahi Tuna and yet they do the best Grilled Cheese Sandwich you'll ever have.

Building upward and outward from its solid foundation of Southern, Cajun, and Southwestern fare, the menu expands into something larger, weirder, more lavish and whimsical—a kind of square-hip soul food that's world-fusion, omni-brow, pan-everything, what-the-hell, and why-not?

Any other restaurant that tried to pull off this sort of eclecticism would collapse in its own confusion. The center simply would not hold. But Harry's Roadhouse revels in confusion, and somehow makes impeccably good sense of it. "We like to have fun with food," Harry says, almost bashfully. "We like a little this-and-that. Whenever we get comfortable with something we say, 'Let's change it!'"

Harry's calls itself a roadhouse, but what does that mean? What is a roadhouse, exactly? It's not quite a diner, though it may have some diner DNA. Nor is it a café, or a drive-in, or a grill, or a BBQ joint, though it may claim genes from any of these sturdy species. A roadhouse does not have a single identifiable look or a single identifiable fare.

So what is it? I think that a roadhouse may be the closest thing we have in our relentlessly mobile society to an English pub. Informal, unpretentious, maybe a little rough around the edges—and maybe, in certain phases of the day, a bit raucous. A loud taverny place where people gather in a regular sort of way. A place where stout spirits are imbibed, to be sure, but also a place for kids and grandpas and crazy old aunts who probably should not be drinking. A kind of community center for restless souls of all ages.

The road part is easy: It's gotta be a spot you drive to, somewhere on the outskirts of town, on the interesting edge between urban and rural. A place of busy comings and goings, where you look out the window at the bustle of the world and where the worldly bustle comes in for a rest. An establishment built up from the filth and grit of the road, but

close enough to benefit from whatever the road has to offer.

The house part is even easier: It's got to feel like home.

Harry's Roadhouse answers all those definitions, and then some. Its roots are emphatically in and of the road. The place itself is located on a pre-1937 branch of Route 66, and it's only a stone's throw from one of the most storied byways in our country's history: the Santa Fe Trail, the old rutted wagon route that once extended all the way to Independence, Missouri, bringing the goods and ideas (and foods) of America to the Great Southwest.

The restaurant was once a gas station, and then a VW repair shop. After that it was the Nifty Café, a funk-a-delic little dive with questionable wiring that boasted "same day service—guaranteed." Even today, Harry's is located on an interesting stretch of asphalt, just down the way from an Indian convenience store, a groovy New Age garden emporium, and a bustling free-form market locally known as "Sticks and Stones," where hawkers sell everything from elk heads to velvet Elvises to enormous lichen-splotched boulders. In other words, it's a great location for a roadhouse—a messily, pleasantly real corridor of multiple transactions, where the prosaic meets the exotic, and where some residual flavor of the old Santa Fe trade lingers.

From all this cluttered madness, you pull into the congested Harry's lot, and there it is—the familiar white stucco pavilion trimmed out in loud turquoise and happy purple paint. Inside the waiting area, the walls are hung with kiddie art—crayonne en papier offerings from the local tots. Some of the art is damn good, and some of it really sucks, but it doesn't matter; the point is there's kid art on the wall, and that sets a certain tone right from the start: Families R Welcome Here. Once, a customer complained about the children two tables over who were singing and generally making a ruckus; instead of shushing the offending kids, Harry said, "Yes, aren't they terrific?"

Inside the restaurant proper, the walls are hung with paintings by artists who happen to be grown-ups. Some of the art is damn good, and some of it really sucks, but again that doesn't matter. The point is, all of these offerings are done by locals—most of them restaurant regulars, in fact—

and so every room of Harry's is chock-full of color and warmth and homegrown cheer. Being native Philadelphians, Harry and Peyton have of course packed their place with brotherly (and sisterly) love.

All the other touches, too, are warm and festive and real: Peyton's immaculate pies and cakes arrayed on the counter, the informal gardens in the back, the bright Mexican oil-cloths, the gnarled cottonwood that seems to grow right into the building, Joel Nakamura's celestial-peyote-trip design along the bar (where the favorite belly-uppin' spot of a now-deceased regular is commemorated by a discreet sign, "Tom stands here").

The cumulative effect of all this is that Harry's does indeed feel like home—and many folks pretty much set up shop there like they own the place. I know people who go there seven days a week and keep an account. I know a few superstitious regulars who refuse to make any important life decision without first downing an order of Peyton's Lucky Pudding, which, they say, has proven cosmic powers. I know people who go to Harry's immediately upon their return from a long trip—I mean, straight from the airport.

"I don't feel like I'm really home until I swing by Harry's," says one of these folks. "Otherwise, I just don't feel grounded."

Yet make no mistake, good atmosphere is not enough; none of us would be coming back again and again and again for mediocre victuals. Ultimately, it's all about great good food, and great good food is what you'll find in these pages. For that reason alone, I think you'll enjoy this book. Eat this blessed fare and I believe you, too, will feel "grounded." Perhaps you can turn your own kitchen into a roadhouse.

But frankly, I think Harry and Peyton are crazy as hell to do this cookbook. It's just a stupid idea to give out all these recipes, and I hate it. Now Roadhouse fans like me will have no more excuses: Armed with this graceful little manual, we'll have to stay home every once in a while . . . and cook for ourselves.

—HAMPTON SIDES, Santa Fe, New Mexico

Hampton Sides is the award-winning author of Blood and Thunder, *a non-fiction Western about the controversial life and times of Kit Carson. His other books include* Americana *and* Ghost Soldiers. *Now an editor-at-large for* Outside *magazine, Hampton lives "just up the hill" from the Roadhouse with his wife, Anne, and their three boys.*

ACKNOWLEDGMENTS

We could never have completed this cookbook and kept the restaurant running smoothly without an outstanding dedicated staff. Our manager Kathleen O'Brien has been in charge of the dining room for over five years and has touched the lives of so many regulars and all of us. Her husband, Michael Carlson, has worked at the Roadhouse in every capacity for about eight years and is currently mixmaster extraordinaire. Brent Lancour, who began as a line cook nine years ago, and now is Chef, has kept the kitchen humming and has been instrumental in developing and testing many of the recipes.

Without the efforts of so many loyal employees, the Roadhouse would not have become the successful restaurant and community center that it is today. In the restaurant business, it is really important to have long-term employees that care. Bucky, Kendra, Linda, Angela, Oliver, Kerry, John Young, Ismael, Javier, Jesus, Daniel and Daniel, Christian, Jaime, Mario, and Jonathan all have been dedicated employees over the past few years, and continue to help us grow. We hope they will be around for a long time to come. Jules, Dayni, Armando, Juana, Caroline, Trista, Rose, Laura, and Ginger all stand out in our minds as people who really helped make the Roadhouse what it is today even though they have moved on to other things.

We also found an extended family of customers who have made the Roadhouse what it is as much as either of us. Claire and Richard have been coming in since we first opened. They are the regular regulars. Claire eats at the Roadhouse every day. She's our spell checker for the specials' board, serves as boot camp for the new wait staff, and makes sure that Harry never serves an ersatz Salad Nicoise. Then we have Don Barliant and Jan Bailey, who have been loyal customers from day one and have given us great counsel over the years.

Everyone deserves to be part of a dream team. We have been lucky enough to work with one on this book. Joe, Jack, Maria, and Hampton all were great customers and friends before we came together for this project. They all had a trove of dining experiences, knew many of our staff members, and understand what makes Harry's Roadhouse tick.

Joel Nakamura is an excellent illustrator and has been an incredible supporter over the years. He painted the bar top in dizzying, out-of-this-world detail. He also draws kids' menus and designs our T-shirts. Sometimes we joke that the restaurant should be called Joel's Roadhouse. But, most of all, he brings happiness to all of us at the Roadhouse by being someone that we all look forward to seeing, especially when he's with his beautiful children, Paloma and Kai, and Kathleen, his wife. Oh, and Joel's parents—they're great!

Jack Kotz, we have known for years. We all knew he was an incredible photographer, but who knew he could make the Roadhouse food look so good in photographs? We just cooked it, and he shot it, and then he and Joel ate it. Occasionally, but rarely, there were leftovers for the staff. Everything for this book was photographed at the Roadhouse right as it came out of the kitchen, without any of the manipulation that is so common in food photography.

Joel told us to get in touch with Maria Levy. As soon as we saw her last book project, we knew that she was the one and that she had to design this book. Maria has always stayed true to our vision. Maria is so easygoing and such a pleasure to work with that it came as a surprise when she started constantly nagging me about when we would be serving Country Gravy with Biscuits again. Who would have thought that a petite Chinese woman, raised in Costa Rica and with the last name of Levy, would get hooked on this truckers' classic?

Hampton Sides, another regular customer, has been a friend since our kids were all in Montessori together. We were shocked that such an inveterate punner would go on to be a successful author writing best-sellers. We are highly appreciative of the fun and quirky introduction he bequeathed to the book.

Rosé is another one of those very special people who found us and adopted us and became a great friend. He is a soup aficionado, a poet, a performance artist, a beat hipster, and an intellectual. He is the kind of man who makes Santa Fe a special place and reminds us how lucky we are to live here. On many occasions he has completed his dining experience at the Roadhouse with one of his special tomes, a couple of which we have included in this book.

Special thanks to the families who allowed us to test out our recipes on them. The Franklins, Barliants, and especially the Hocketts, who allowed us to christen their new kitchen in Virginia with sea level baking experiments. Also, Leanna Coppola and Zoe for their efforts in helping me perfect lots of baked goods after school.

PEYTON YOUNG, ZOE, AND HARRY SHAPIRO

INTRODUCTION

A WORD FROM HARRY

A little story about a graduate student who wanted to impress his friends at their weekend party (it seemed that everyone else knew how to cook): He decided to cook fried chicken, pulled out *The Fannie Farmer Cookbook* that everyone told him was the Whole Earth Catalog for beginning cooks, and started the meal. Well, there was no corn oil in the house so he assumed that he could just substitute corn syrup. The raw chicken hardened in the hot corn syrup and the whole mess, pan and all, ended up in the trash. I don't remember if they had KFC or if they skipped the food and went on to the "main course." It was 1970 after all. Clueless? Yes. Stupid? Yes. Hopeless? Not at all.

I am sure that you have guessed by now that that "challenged" young man was none other than yours truly. Undaunted, over the next ten years, cooking became somewhat of a hobby. I improved and had no mishaps that rivaled that one, but continued to have my share of disasters. In 1972, I came home from a trip to the Southwest with a big bag of New Mexico red chiles. Here was something new and exotic, something that I wanted to learn to use. This became one of my passions—learning to cook with chiles.

In 1980, I decided to pursue cooking professionally and in the twenty-five plus years that have followed, hopefully I have learned a thing or two. What can I share with you in this day and age of the sophisticated palate, thousands of fine cookbooks, and a twenty-four hour food channel? Can any of us compete with Emeril, Mario, and the likes? They sure intimidate me. Now Julia Childs, she was real. She let it all hang out—quirks, eccentricities, and, most importantly, mistakes. Because the deepest, darkest secret of professional cooking is that we all make them. We are just better at covering them up, or at blaming them on a sous chef or purveyor.

So this it what I have to say to you:

★ Engage your senses—whether you are shopping or chopping. Wake up and smell, touch, and listen to the sizzle. And taste, taste, taste every step of the way! When your mom told you not to play with your food, you were a kid. Now that you are a serious, mature human being it is time to relearn this enlightened habit.

★ Cook to have fun—after all, cooking is a recreation and should be pleasurable. It is not your job. Learn to enjoy your weekend or evening. If you are reading this book, you are pursuing cooking as a pastime. You could be playing golf, gardening, skydiving, biking, or skiing, but you have chosen to cook. Relax and enjoy it.

★ When you entertain and cook for others you are giving a real gift, something from your heart.

★ Cook what you like; don't cook to impress your guests.

★ Learn to accept your inevitable mistakes with humor and learn from them.

A WORD FROM PEYTON

When I was a kid in the '70s, going out to dinner was a big deal. My mom, dad, and I would all get dressed up and order fancy food like Filet with Bearnaise Sauce or Chicken Kiev. Dessert would be something like Chocolate Mousse or Coeur a la Crème. It was always a festive occasion. Things really changed for me in the '80s. My parents got divorced, and I moved from the suburbs of Philadelphia to Center City Philadelphia. My mother went to The Philadelphia Restaurant School and became a chef and restaurant manager. Instead of eating out being a special occasion, I lived the reverse. Eating at home was a special occasion where we would cook a celebratory meal and linger over the preparation and eating. Many times we ate our meals where my mother was working, and the other employees became our friends and family. I'd stop by after school or for dinner if my mom had to work late. But we ate out at lots of other places too. Diners for breakfast, where Nice Mary served you "nice pancakes." Ethnic restaurants for pasta in South Philly, Vietnamese and Thai in Chinatown, Middle Eastern for a falafel fix. Local neighborhood spots where you knew the staff and they took special care of you. Living in a big city you could always find a variety of great food at reasonable prices, whatever you craved.

When we moved to Santa Fe, we found there were a lot of excellent high-end restaurants and a lot of New Mexican food, but not a lot in between. The little building on the Old Las Vegas Highway seemed too far out of town to be a real neighborhood spot to me, but I was wrong. The building had been a gas station on the old Route 66, a Volkswagen repair shop, then a series of funky restaurants. The community around us has grown by leaps and bounds.

And the Roadhouse has become a community center. We have people who eat there once or twice a week and people who are in the restaurant three times a day many days. Some people order the same thing every time they come. Other people make it a point to come on Tuesday nights when we change the specials for the week.

As Harry likes to say, we feel we have inherited a spot with its own history, energy, and good will, and we feel lucky to be caretakers of this very special place.

Rhythms

A DAY AT HARRY'S: 24/7, NOT QUITE, BUT 18/7, ALWAYS

Bleary eyed at 6:00 a.m. the first shift is arriving, but already on the loading dock are cases of food ordered the day before. Coffee is on the way for the groggy staff, but there are always one or two larks who are already in high gear. We open at 7:00 a.m. By then everyone and everything has to be ready—muffins, pancake and waffle batters, and lots of coffee. Early morning, the Roadhouse smells of bacon and coffee. On weekends the bakers are rushing to get the cinnamon rolls out. The cooks are preparing the menu items, plus two or three egg specials, and two more pancake, waffle, or french toast specials. By 7:00 a.m., the chairs are down, the tables are set, the doors unlocked, the sign is turned, and the staff is sufficiently caffeinated. We are ready! Here it comes . . .

It's 9:00 p.m., 14 hours later, and a long day is winding down. The staff is starting to eat dinner in shifts. The crowds are thinning; the cooks are eager to get in the last orders so that they can start to clean and go home (or go wherever). A few people are at the bar arguing with Oliver, our resident Republican. Kathleen is "cracking the whip" trying to keep the night staff focused. The restaurant's day will finally end sometime between 11:00 p.m. and midnight, after the bar has been restocked, the kitchen has been cleaned, all of the floors have been hosed and mopped, and the deposits have been made. After a six hour break we will start all over again.

But the middle, what about the middle? Breakfast to lunch, lunch all afternoon until dinner, with no breaks, staff changing over, and customers coming and going throughout. Depending on the season and the day, anywhere from 500 to 1,100 customers will have come through the doors—families with kids, people who work in the neighborhood, local residents, tourists, people with second homes, but mostly regulars.

Regulars (return customers) fuel the Roadhouse. We don't advertise and have a simple philosophy: **Happy customers return.** Do whatever you can to make sure that everyone leaves looking forward to their next visit. That's the challenge and the pleasure. I am always in awe of the bonds between the staff and customers, management and staff and ex-staff who have moved on but are still in touch. At any moment, I probably know 30 to 50 percent of the customers, and I spend most of my time in the kitchen. Kathleen, Angela, Micheal, and Linda all know a lot more of them than I do.

To say that the Roadhouse has exceeded my expectations is an understatement, not just business-wise, but in becoming a community institution. Every time someone comes in and says,

"How do you do it? Everyone is working so hard, but they are all laughing, joking, and having so much fun?"

"Where do you come up with all of those specials?"

"We just got back into town. We haven't been home yet because we don't feel like we are back in Santa Fe until we have eaten at Harry's."

"These are my [friends, family] from out of town and this is the first place that we wanted to take them."

. . . I feel like the luckiest guy in the world.

—Harry Shapiro

HARRY'S ROADHOUSE

I dined again at Harry's yesterday
Which just completely knocked me for a loop
I eat there all the time, what can I say
Except this meal was headline news, a scoop
A feast to resurrect a dead gourmet
We started with Italian wedding soup
Mysteriously intricate, subtle and rich
With lightly spicy meatballs that made our taste buds twitch

And after soup was whisked away despite
My efforts to lap up each single drop
Because it filled my soul with such delight
And made me want to sip and never stop
A salad was brought in made of starlight
And spinach leaves and dancing on the top
Blood oranges and roasted beets, smiling, looking gladdish
Tossed together in a sauce of citrus and horseradish

Without fanfare there enters now a dish
Of capellini formed into a nest
Where lies a fine fillet of a monkfish
All glistening and looking self-possessed
As grand as anything that you might wish
Each mouthful tasting like it had been blest
Did I forget the capers, sprinkled all around
That burst on tongue like sparkling stars and render me spellbound?

To cap this stellar meal, make it complete
Put the proverbial icing on the cake
To finish off the dinner with a sweet
Our host at Harry's set their team to bake
An apple pie to make all others obsolete
A pie for which the world you would forsake
Whose tasty crust and luscious fruit is like a dream
That never ends, just endless apple pie and cream.

— *Rosé*

Roadhouse Basics

At the Roadhouse we do quite a bit of traditional Mexican cooking. The roasting of chiles, peppers, onion, garlic, herbs, spices, and corn are frequently repeated in a variety of recipes throughout the book. This roasting process concentrates flavors and adds a little rustic "open flame" element to the completed dish.

GREEN CHILES AND PEPPERS

At home, roast on an outdoor grill or right over a gas burner. Just set the pepper right on an open flame. When the outside layer starts to blister away from the meat of the pepper, turn it so that the raw side is facing the flame. When blistered all over, simply place the pepper in a plastic bag. The bags that are in rolls in the produce section of your local market are perfect. Twist the bag tightly around the peppers and set aside for about 15 minutes. Remove the peppers from bag and peel off the outside blistered layer. Open up the pepper and remove the seed and veins. For poblano chiles and other thin-skinned peppers, brush on a light coat of oil before roasting them. This accelerates the charring process and prevents the meaty part of the pepper from getting overcooked. If you have sensitive skin, you may want to use rubber gloves when peeling chiles.

GARLIC, ONIONS, AND TOMATOES

Traditionally onions and garlic are roasted on a comal, which is a piece of sheet metal placed over hot coals. At home I use a cast-iron pan. Heat the pan and place garlic (whole heads are perfect) over a medium-high heat. Do not peel the garlic. Turn until toasted. Be careful as a little charring is fine, but burnt garlic has a bitterness that will permeate the finished dish. For onions, I cut each onion and into four to six wedges and toast in the pan until the onion is cooked almost through. Onions are more forgiving than garlic and a little dark char on the outside of the onion will just add depth to the finished product. Tomatoes can simply be thrown into the pan whole and turned until they are lightly charred on all sides. Let onions and garlic cool, then peel. Tomatoes can be used whole.

HERBS AND SPICES

Toast in a small sauté pan over medium-high heat. Be careful not to burn and char the spices. Since the pan will stay hot, remove herbs and spices from the pan immediately when they are ready. Toast individual herbs and spices separately since they all have different cooking times. Oregano and cloves will toast very quickly, while canela takes quite a bit more time.

ROASTING CORN

The simplest way to roast corn outside is to sprinkle a little water on an unhusked ear, wrap it in foil, and roast right on the coals, just like you would bake a potato. Usually this takes about 20 minutes. Indoors, simply preheat an oven to 350 degrees F, sprinkle water on corn in husk, and place on a sheet pan (you do not need to wrap ears in foil). Roast in oven for about 30 minutes.

TORTILLA STRIPS

For Migas, Sopa de Lima, and other dishes, we like to make our own corn tortilla strips. Start by cutting the tortillas in half and then cutting across the tortilla, creating fettuccine-like strips. Fry these in hot vegetable oil for about 1½ to 2 minutes. Test a strip; when it is crunchy, remove all of the strips and drain on paper towels. These strips can be used in place of croutons to add crunch to a salad. A good quality tortilla strip can always be substituted.

PREPARING TORTILLAS FOR ENCHILADAS

Corn tortillas must be soft and pliable in order to correctly roll an enchilada and properly absorb sauce. The preparation is simple and straightforward. Have a plate or mixing bowl ready with a ½ cup of enchilada sauce. Heat ¼ inch of vegetable oil in an 8-inch sauté pan to 350 degrees F. Fry each tortilla in oil for about 15 seconds, turn, and cook the other side for about 10 seconds. Remove the tortilla with a pair of tongs. If you have cooked the tortilla enough, it should be soft and flexible. If it is falling apart, then it is overcooked. Hold vertically with tongs and let excess oil drain back into the sauté pan. Pat with a paper towel and while hot, coat both sides with enchilada sauce by briefly dipping the tortilla into sauce. Stuff and roll immediately. The enchiladas can be held for later use at this point. To keep the tortillas from drying out and cracking, cover with a clean, damp kitchen towel. White or yellow corn enchiladas are better than blue corn enchiladas for rolling. In New Mexico, where blue corn tortillas are traditional, the enchiladas are stacked.

DRY CHILES

Toast dry chiles in a cast-iron pan over medium-high heat. Turn after about 1 minute and toast the other side. The idea is to bring the chiles to life, not to char or burn them. Remove and soak chiles in water overnight. You may accelerate this process by placing the chiles in a pot and covering them with water. Bring the water to a boil and turn off heat, then cover the pot. Let the chiles sit for about 30 minutes. The amount of time it takes to reconstitute a chile will depend on the type of chile and how fresh it is. When it is ready to use, it should be soft and pliable, but not falling apart. Remove the stems and seeds and drain off excess liquid. Again, if your skin is sensitive to chiles, you may want to wear rubber gloves. In general, the soaking liquid is discarded.

SALSAS

Most salsas will thicken over time. A salsa that has the perfect consistency when you make it may be too thick when you are ready to serve it. Just add a little stock or water and taste. Usually you will want to add a little more salt to bring the flavor back into balance.

PLANTAINS

Use only ripe plantains. They will look black and ugly. Peel and cut them into 1½-inch rounds. Fry in vegetable oil at a medium heat (300 degrees F) until they are soft all the way through. This should take 3 to 4 minutes. Remove and drain. Take the flat side of a chef's knife or a salad plate and press down, smashing the plantain until it is about ¼ inch thick. Fry a second time in oil heated to 350 degrees F until the plantains start to turn a golden color. Drain and serve.

DESSERTS

DOUBLE CHOCOLATE ESPRESSO BROWNIES 20

CHOCOLATE BREAD PUDDING 22

BOURBON-PECAN CARAMEL SAUCE 22

ZOE'S POTS DE CRÈME 23

LUCKY PUDDING 24

CHOCOLATE CHUNK COOKIES 27

VANILLA PANNA COTTA 27

BUTTERSCOTCH CUSTARD WITH CHOCOLATE-ORANGE SAUCE 28

PIE DOUGH 29

APPLE PIE 31

PECAN PIE 31

COCONUT CREAM PIE 32

WHITE CHOCOLATE BANANA CREAM PIE 33

LEMON MERINGUE PIE 34

STRAWBERRY-RHUBARB PIE 37

PUMPKIN PIE 37

BLUEBERRY PIE 38

APRICOT-BLACKBERRY CRISP 41

CRISP TOPPING 41

PEACH COBBLER 41

GERMAN CHOCOLATE CAKE 42–43

ECLAIRS 44–45

FLOURLESS CHOCOLATE CAKE 45

4 ounces unsweetened
   chocolate

½ cup (1 stick) butter

1 tablespoon espresso or
   strong brewed coffee*

3 eggs

½ teaspoon salt

1½ cups sugar

1 cup flour

1 ounce semisweet
   chocolate, chopped

¼ cup chopped walnuts

*You can substitute instant
espresso powder.*

DOUBLE CHOCOLATE ESPRESSO BROWNIES

PREP TIME: 20 minutes

BAKING TIME: 25 minutes

FEEDS: 6

Melt unsweetened chocolate and butter in a double boiler or microwave. (If you use a microwave, be careful not to let the chocolate burn. Heat for 30 seconds, remove, and stir. Heat 30 seconds more. The chocolate should be smooth but not hot.) Add espresso or strong brewed coffee.

In a mixing bowl with a whisk attachment, beat eggs with salt until foamy. Add sugar and beat on high for 5 minutes, until mixture doubles in volume. Put chocolate mixture in a large bowl. Fold in egg mixture. Combine until smooth, but try not to depress the egg volume. Sift in the flour and fold until batter is smooth. Fold in semisweet chocolate chunks and nuts.

Spray a 9- x 9-inch pan with nonstick cooking spray. Pour batter into prepared pan and bake for 25 minutes at 350 degrees F. After they cool, cut brownies to desired size.

These are incredibly rich and fudge-like. A little goes a long way. I love them warm with some ice cream. One of our most popular desserts is a Brownie Sundae with Hot Fudge, Pecan-Bourbon Caramel Sauce, Vanilla Häagen Dazs ice cream, and whipped cream. The sundae is a big dessert perfect for sharing.

DOUBLE CHOCOLATE ESPRESSO BROWNIES

CHOCOLATE BREAD PUDDING

PREP TIME: 20 minutes

BAKING TIME: 55 minutes

FEEDS: 9

1 (1-pound) loaf rustic
    bread
2 cups milk
2 cups heavy cream
1 cup sugar
8 eggs
1 teaspoon vanilla
1 teaspoon almond extract
8 ounces semisweet
    chocolate, chopped

Remove the crust from bread and discard. Cut bread into small (1-inch) squares.

Put the milk, cream, and sugar in a saucepan and scald. Meanwhile, beat eggs, vanilla, and almond extract together in a large bowl with a whisk until smooth. When the milk is scalded, remove it from the heat and add chopped chocolate. Let the chocolate dissolve, whisking occasionally. Then slowly add the chocolate milk to the whipped eggs, whisking as you pour in the milk.

Add the bread cubes to the custard; mix well and let bread absorb liquid for 1 hour, stirring occasionally. Pour pudding into a greased 9- x 12-inch pan and bake for 45 minutes, covered with foil, at 325 degrees F. Remove foil and bake 10 more minutes.

BOURBON-PECAN CARAMEL SAUCE

PREP TIME: 10 minutes

COOKING TIME: 25 minutes

1½ cups sugar
⅓ cup corn syrup
2 teaspoons lemon juice
1 cup heavy cream
2 tablespoons bourbon
½ cup pecans, toasted and
    chopped

In a large heavy saucepan, mix sugar and corn syrup. Watching carefully, bring the sugar mixture to a boil and let it caramelize. You'll know it's ready when you can smell burnt sugar and the mixture is a caramel color with a smooth consistency. Add lemon juice to stop the caramelizing process.

Slowly pour in cream; it will boil up, so be careful. Bring the mixture back to a boil and then turn down to a simmer. Let it cook for 5 minutes. Remove from heat and cool for 10 minutes; then add bourbon and pecans. Now the sauce is ready to serve, or it can be cooled and reheated later. Any extra can be refrigerated for later use.

ZOE'S POTS DE CRÈME

PREP TIME: 15 minutes

COOKING TIME: 1 to 1½ hours

CHILLING TIME: 2 hours

FEEDS: 6

1½ cups heavy cream
1 cup milk
½ cup sugar
8 ounces semisweet
   chocolate, chopped
8 egg yolks
1 teaspoon vanilla

This dessert is very simple to make, but you need patience to cook it right. I begin checking for doneness after 1 hour in the oven, but it usually takes an hour and a half. After cooking, you need to chill the custards for 2 more hours until they are good and cold. I like to sprinkle the tops with vanilla sugar (see page 44).

This is one of our daughter's favorite desserts and what she always requests for a special dinner or when she gets a good report card.

Bring cream, milk, and sugar to a boil in a medium saucepan. Melt the chopped chocolate in the cream. Whisk egg yolks and then slowly drizzle the chocolate cream into the yolks. Keep whisking as you slowly add the hot cream. When combined, pour through a sieve into a pitcher and add vanilla. Pour into 6 ramekins.

Place ramekins in a 9- x 13-inch pan with 2-to-3-inch sides and fill with water until it is halfway up the sides of the ramekins. Cover with foil and bake in the oven at 275 degrees F. These bake slowly over a long period of time. Check after 1 hour, but it will probably be 1 hour and 30 minutes before they are set. Remove from oven. Cool to room temperature and then chill. Serve with whipped cream.

Baking puddings in a water bath helps slow down the cooking so the egg does not curdle. But you must watch them closely.

Jiggle the dishes. If they are still watery in the middle, they need more time. It's good to check every 5 minutes. They will jiggle but will be firm in the middle when they are set.

**BUTTERSCOTCH
PUDDING**
2 cups milk, divided
3 tablespoons cornstarch
2 egg yolks
½ cup brown sugar
½ teaspoon vanilla
1 tablespoon butter
¼ teaspoon salt

CHOCOLATE PUDDING
2 cups milk, divided
2 ounces unsweetened
    chocolate
2 tablespoons cornstarch
2 egg yolks
5 tablespoons sugar
½ teaspoon vanilla
1 tablespoon butter
Pinch salt

LUCKY PUDDING

PREP TIME: 15 minutes
COOKING TIME: 10 minutes
CHILLING TIME: 3 hours
FEEDS: 4

To make the Butterscotch Pudding: Put 1½ cups milk in a saucepan over medium-high heat and bring to the scalding point. Meanwhile, mix the other ½ cup of milk with the cornstarch, egg yolks, and brown sugar in another pan. Slowly add the scalded milk to the cornstarch mixture. When combined, return to the stovetop and whisk over medium heat until thickened. Remove from heat and add vanilla, butter, and salt. Pour through a sieve into a bowl and cover with plastic wrap. Chill for 2 hours or until cold all the way through. You can speed up this process with an ice bath.

To make the Chocolate Pudding: Put 1½ cups milk in a saucepan over medium-high heat and bring to the scalding point. Chop chocolate and add it to the milk; remove from heat. Stir chocolate and milk until smooth. Meanwhile, mix the other ½ cup of milk with the cornstarch, egg yolks, and sugar. Add to the scalded milk and whisk over medium heat until thickened. Remove from heat and add vanilla, butter, and salt. Pour through a sieve, into a bowl and cover with plastic wrap. Chill 2 hours or until cold all the way through.

When chilled, alternately layer the Butterscotch and Chocolate Puddings in four parfait glasses until filled. Top with whipped cream.

This is Joel Nakamura's special pudding. (Joel is the illustrator of this book.) It got its name "lucky" because Joel claims that if he eats it before he has a softball game, he plays great and his team wins.

Joel and some of his friends even claim that some big deals have been made after eating this pudding. I like to think Lucky Pudding was responsible for Joel's son Kai, but who knows?

CHOCOLATE CHUNK COOKIES

CHOCOLATE CHUNK COOKIES

PREP TIME: 15 minutes

BAKING TIME: 13 minutes

FEEDS: Makes 2 dozen 3-inch cookies

1 cup butter

1 cup sugar

1½ cups brown sugar

1 tablespoon vanilla

4 eggs

4 cups flour

2 teaspoons baking soda

1 teaspoon salt

12 ounces semisweet chocolate, chopped

Beat butter, sugar, brown sugar, and vanilla in a large mixing bowl at high speed. When fluffy, add the eggs, one at a time. Mix together the dry ingredients separately. Add dry ingredients to the egg mixture in two additions. Mix in the chopped chocolate, but do not overmix. Portion out cookies by quarter cups on a cookie sheet lined with parchment paper. Bake for 10 minutes at 350 degrees F. Remove the cookie sheet from the oven and slap it on a counter to make the cookies fall. Return cookie sheet to the oven and bake for 2 minutes more. Serve with milk.

Note: At sea level, add 4 tablespoons more butter and ¼ cup more sugar, and reduce the flour to 3½ cups.

VANILLA PANNA COTTA

PREP TIME: 15 minutes

CHILLING TIME: 4 hours

FEEDS: 4

½ tablespoon gelatin

2 tablespoons water

2½ cups half-and-half

½ cup sugar

⅓ vanilla bean

In a large bowl, dissolve gelatin in water. In a saucepan, heat the half-and-half with sugar and the vanilla bean. Bring to a simmer and then remove from stove. Remove the vanilla bean and split it open. Scrape the seeds into the custard. Keep the vanilla bean for making vanilla sugar (see page 44). Slowly pour the half-and-half mixture over the gelatin mixture and whisk until smooth. Pour into flan dishes and chill until set, about 4 hours.

We started making panna cottas in our continuous search for egg-free and citrus-free desserts for regular customer Janet Bailey. This has proven to be a great addition to the menu. Panna cottas are egg-free custards thickened with gelatin. This makes them creamy but light. They are perfect on a warm day with fresh berries, or in the winter with fruit sauce and a cookie.

BUTTERSCOTCH CUSTARD WITH CHOCOLATE-ORANGE SAUCE

PREP TIME: 30 minutes

COOKING TIME: 45 minutes

CHILLING TIME: 2 hours

FEEDS: 6

BUTTERSCOTCH CUSTARD

¾ cup sugar

¼ cup water

1 cup milk

2 cups heavy cream

¼ cup brown sugar

6 egg yolks

CHOCOLATE-ORANGE SAUCE

¼ cup heavy cream

2 tablespoons sugar

1½ ounces semisweet chocolate, chopped

½ tablespoon butter

1 teaspoon Triple Sec or orange extract

To make the Butterscotch Custard:
Caramelize sugar and water in a non-reactive pan by cooking over high heat until the sugar has a burnt sugar smell and golden brown color.

Meanwhile, heat milk, cream, and brown sugar in a saucepan over medium heat, stirring to combine as the sugar dissolves.

Put egg yolks in a large bowl with a bowl of ice below it.

When the caramelized sugar is ready, slowly add hot milk mixture. It will bubble up, so be careful. Turn off the heat and stir the mixture until all the caramel is incorporated into the hot milk. Then slowly ladle hot mixture into egg yolks, whisking continuously. Keep adding and mixing slowly. When finished mixing, pour custard through a sieve. Fill flan dishes or ramekins with custard and set them in a 9- x 13-inch pan filled with hot water so that the water goes halfway up the sides of the dishes. Cover pan with foil and bake for 45 minutes at 325 degrees F. Make sure puddings are set. Bake longer if necessary, checking every 5 minutes. Take dishes out of water bath and chill for 2 hours. Drizzle with Chocolate-Orange Sauce.

To make the Chocolate-Orange Sauce:
Combine cream and sugar in a small saucepan and bring to a simmer. Add chocolate to the hot cream; stir until smooth. Then add butter and Triple Sec or orange extract. Prepare ahead of time but keep at room temperature. Drizzle onto Butterscotch Custards.

Many of our bakers over the years have added recipes to the Harry's repertoire. One of our favorites is this custard from Caroline Huggins, who has since become an English teacher. It has been very popular at the Roadhouse ever since she introduced it.

PIE DOUGH

PREP TIME: 20 minutes

CHILLING TIME: 30 minutes

4 cups pastry flour
½ teaspoon salt
10 tablespoons margarine
10 tablespoons shortening
1 cup ice water (with ice removed)

This is the pie dough recipe we have used since day one at the restaurant. A very accomplished baker (and good friend and teacher) Karen English showed it to me when she was teaching me how to bake. There's much debate about what fat to use in your pie dough. Many cooks use lard or butter. I suggest experimenting and seeing what tastes best to you.

We get a lot of compliments on our piecrust, so we've opted to stick with it. It's very easy to make but takes getting used to how the dough should look and feel through the various steps. You want to incorporate the cold fat until the flour has a crumbly texture without big lumps of fat, but you cannot let it go too far or it will become a ball of dough and you will not be able to incorporate the ice water. You want to have the ice water ready to go and do it all at once. This will keep the dough from becoming too wet. Continue mixing the dough just until it comes together and is smooth, with all the flour from the bottom of the bowl fully incorporated.

Get all ingredients ready. Keep margarine, shortening, and ice water cold. Mix together flour and salt. Cut up margarine and shortening into small pieces.

Using an electric mixer is the easy way to go, but people have been making pie dough for centuries without a mixer. Either way, cut the margarine and shortening into the flour until it is crumbly like cornmeal, without a lot of big chunks of fat. Then add ice water, all at once, to the dough.

Continue mixing until the dough seems fairly smooth. (We often pull the dough off the paddle at this point, throw in a small handful of flour, and then beat it again for a few seconds. This seems to smooth out the dough a little more and make it easy to work with.) As with all dough, avoid overworking it, because it will become tough if you do.

Divide dough into three portions and flatten into disc shapes. Wrap with plastic wrap and chill for 30 minutes. You can freeze any extra dough at this point for a later use. After chilling, roll out dough and follow directions for the pie you are making.

NOTE ON PIES: I did not find any need to adjust pie ingredients at sea level; however, the cooking times will be longer. The fruit juice should be bubbling and thick before removing pies from the oven. If your crust seems to be getting too brown, protect it with some foil while allowing the filling to cook longer. Fillings are done when the liquid has thickened and is bubbling.

CLOCKWISE: APPLE PIE, COCONUT CREAM PIE, WHITE CHOCOLATE BANANA CREAM PIE, STRAWBERRY-RHUBARB PIE, AND PECAN PIE

APPLE PIE

PREP TIME: 15 minutes

COOKING TIME: 45 minutes or until fruit liquid is bubbling and thick

FEEDS: 6

13 Granny Smith apples
1 cup brown sugar
2 teaspoons cinnamon
3 tablespoons cornstarch
2 tablespoons butter, chilled
¼ cup bourbon
Pie Dough for 2 crusts
(see recipe on page 29)
Egg wash (1 egg whisked
with 2 tablespoons water)
¼ cup cinnamon-sugar
mixture

Core, peel, and slice apples. Mix apples, brown sugar, cinnamon, and cornstarch; add to saucepan with butter and cook over medium-high heat until just tender. Remove from heat and add bourbon. Let cool. Roll out pie dough for 9-inch pie pan. Line bottom of pan with one pie dough round. Top with cooled apple filling. Cover with second pie dough round. Crimp edges and brush top of pie with egg wash. Make slits in top of crust for vents and sprinkle with cinnamon-sugar. Bake for 1 hour. Test apples for doneness before removing pie from oven. They will be tender to a knife and the filling will be bubbling and look thickened.

PECAN PIE

PREP TIME: 15 minutes

COOKING TIME: 45 minutes

FEEDS: 6

Pie Dough for 1 crust
(see recipe on page 29)
4 eggs
1 cup brown sugar
3 teaspoons vanilla
⅓ cup butter, melted
2 tablespoons bourbon
¾ cup corn syrup
½ cup pancake syrup
½ teaspoon salt
1½ cups pecans

Roll out pie dough and place into a 9-inch pie pan. In a large bowl, mix with a whisk eggs, brown sugar, vanilla, butter, bourbon, corn syrup, pancake syrup, and salt until smooth. Layer pecans in the bottom of the pie shell. Pour the brown sugar mixture over the pecans. Bake the pie for 45 minutes or until it seems set. Remove from oven when there is very little wobble to the filling. Let cool for 15 minutes before serving.

31

Pie Dough for 1 crust
   (see recipe on page 29)
3 cups milk, divided
2 teaspoons gelatin
1 egg
3 egg yolks
¼ cup cornstarch
½ cup sugar
2 tablespoons butter
 1 teaspoon vanilla
½ teaspoon salt
2 cups shredded coconut
1 cup heavy cream
¼ cup toasted coconut

Coconut Cream Pie

PREP TIME: 30 minutes

TURNOUT TIME: 4 hours

FEEDS: 6

Prebake 1 pie shell and set aside.

Put ½ cup milk in a bowl and add gelatin. Let it dissolve for a minute. Add egg, egg yolks, cornstarch, and sugar to the ½ cup of milk with gelatin. Mix well. Put remaining 2½ cups milk in a nonreactive saucepan over high heat to scald the milk. When milk is scalded, slowly add it to the gelatin mixture in the bowl and whisk until incorporated. Then pour mixture back into the pan and return to the stove, whisking all the time. When the mixture begins to boil, remove from heat and add butter, vanilla, salt, and coconut. Whisk until all the butter is melted and incorporated. Then place custard in a container to cool. Cover with plastic wrap against the custard to keep a skin from forming. Chill in the fridge for a few hours or overnight.

Whip cream until stiff peaks form. Fold into the chilled custard until smooth. Try not to overmix. Put mix into prebaked pie shell and top with toasted coconut.

To precook the pie shell, roll out pie dough, fit into a 9-inch pie pan, and place a pie weight in the shell. Or you can fill a coffee filter or foil with dry beans (and spray bottom with nonstick cooking spray) and fit into the uncooked pie shell. Bake at 325 degrees F for 15 minutes. Remove the weight and bake another 5 minutes or until shell is golden brown. Remove from oven and set aside to cool.

White Chocolate Banana Cream Pie

PREP TIME: 30 minutes

TURNOUT TIME: 4 hours

FEEDS: 6

Prebake 1 pie shell according to directions on page 32; set aside.

Place ½ cup milk in a bowl and add gelatin. Let it dissolve for a few minutes. Add egg, egg yolks, cornstarch, and sugar to the milk with gelatin. Mix well. Heat remaining 1½ cups milk in a nonreactive saucepan over medium-high heat. Bring milk in the saucepan to a simmer; then remove from heat. Pour the hot milk slowly into gelatin mixture, while whisking. Then return mixture to the saucepan and heat over high heat. When the mixture comes to a boil and thickens, remove from stove. Add white chocolate and stir until dissolved; then add vanilla. Toss sliced bananas in lemon juice and then place in the bottom of the prebaked pie shell. Pour custard over bananas. Cover with plastic wrap against the custard to prevent a skin from forming. Cool in the fridge for a few hours or overnight.

Right before serving, whip cream with powdered sugar until stiff peaks form. Place topping on cooled pie. Garnish with white chocolate curls.

> The best way to make curls is to use a piece of chocolate that is on the warm side. You can heat it in the microwave for 5 seconds or just let it sit in a warm area of the kitchen. Be careful not to overheat it. Use a peeler to make the curls and drop them over the top of the pie as you peel them off the chocolate block.

PIE
Pie Dough for 1 crust
   (see recipe on page 29)
2 cups milk, divided
1½ teaspoons gelatin
1 egg
2 egg yolks
1½ tablespoons cornstarch
¼ cup sugar
4 ounces white chocolate, chopped
1 teaspoon vanilla
3 bananas, sliced
1 teaspoon lemon juice

TOPPING
1½ cups heavy cream
¾ cup powdered sugar
White chocolate curls

STABILIZER
1 tablespoon cornstarch
2 tablespoons sugar
½ cup water

PIE
Pie Dough for 1 crust
    (see recipe on page 29)
¼ cup cornstarch
1 cup water
¾ cup sugar
7 egg whites
7 egg yolks
¾ cup lemon juice
Zest of 1 lemon
1 tablespoon butter
1 teaspoon cream of tartar
½ cup sugar

LEMON MERINGUE PIE

PREP TIME: 20 minutes
COOKING TIME: 20 minutes
CHILLING TIME: 1½ hours
FEEDS: 6

This pie is a real crowd pleaser. It is, however, temperamental. Do not even try to make it on a humid or rainy day! Meringues tend to weep in this kind of weather. Have all your ingredients ready to go before making the filling and meringue. Use a nonreactive aluminum pan to make the filling so that it does not turn green.

Prebake 1 pie shell according to directions on page 32 and set aside.

Make a stabilizer for the egg whites in a sauté pan by cooking 1 tablespoon cornstarch, 2 tablespoons sugar, and ½ cup water over medium heat until thickened. Set aside until you whip the egg whites. It should not be hot when you add it to the whites.

Mix the ¼ cup cornstarch, 1 cup water, and ¾ cup sugar in a nonreactive pan. Cook over medium-high heat, stirring frequently. Meanwhile, put egg whites into the clean, grease-free bowl of a mixer. Mix egg yolks, lemon juice, and lemon zest together in a separate bowl. When the cornstarch mixture begins to thicken and boil, whisk in the lemon juice mixture. Bring to a boil, stirring constantly. Make sure custard has reached a boil and has begun to thicken, and then cook for 30 seconds more while whisking continuously to prevent burning on the bottom. Remove from heat and add butter. Stir until incorporated.

As soon as filling is off the stove, begin beating egg whites at a low speed. As they begin to froth, add cream of tartar. Then beat at a higher speed until they begin to whiten. At this point, slowly add ½ cup sugar. As the whites begin to stiffen and get fluffy, add the stabilizer you made earlier. Continue to beat until stiff but not dry. Turn the mixer to high. Beat egg whites until they form stiff peaks but are not grainy or dry.

Pour lemon custard into prebaked pie shell. Top with meringue and create a seal around the edges with the meringue against the pie shell edge. Bake for 10 minutes at 325 degrees F, until meringue is golden brown.

Remove pie from oven and let cool at room temperature for half an hour. Refrigerate for 1 hour before serving.

TIPS FOR MAKING GREAT MERINGUES

One important element in making meringues the right way is to have clean egg whites. I always wash and dry my hands before separating eggs. If you get a little yolk in the whites, you can use the broken shell to remove it. Be sure to get all of it, and add another egg white if necessary. It's easier to separate eggs when they are cold, but better to whip them when they are at room temperature. So, separate your eggs before you prebake your pie shell. And then let the whites warm up a little to room temperature before whipping them. The stabilizer included here is a new addition that came from Susan G. Purdy, a cookbook writer extraordinaire, who recently published *Pie in the Sky: Successful Baking at High Altitudes.*

STRAWBERRY-RHUBARB PIE

STRAWBERRY-RHUBARB PIE

PREP TIME: 30 minutes

COOKING TIME: 45 to 60 minutes

FEEDS: 6

1 pint strawberries, rinsed and sliced

4 cups rhubarb, sliced to ½-inch thickness

¾ cup sugar

Juice and zest of 1 orange

¼ cup cornstarch

Pie Dough for 2 crusts (see recipe on page 29)

Egg wash (1 egg whisked with 2 tablespoons water)

3 tablespoons sugar

Mix strawberries, rhubarb, sugar, orange juice, orange zest, and cornstarch in a large bowl. Roll out pie dough for bottom crust and fit into the bottom of a 9-inch pie pan. Place filling in the shell. To make a lattice crust for the top, roll out dough into a rectangular shape and cut into eight 1-inch-wide strips with a knife or pastry cutter. Make a woven pattern over the top of the pie beginning with the two longest strips crossed in the middle and continuing to weave outward toward the edges. Then crimp the edges. Brush egg wash on lattice and around edge of shell. Dust with remaining 3 tablespoons sugar. Bake for 45 minutes to 1 hour at 325 degrees F until fruit is bubbly and thickened.

PUMPKIN PIE

PREP TIME: 30 minutes

COOKING TIME: 40 minutes

FEEDS: 6

Pie Dough for 1 crust (see recipe on page 29)

2 eggs

1 tablespoon brandy

2 cups fresh pumpkin puree

¼ cup brown sugar

¼ cup maple syrup

1 teaspoon cinnamon

1 teaspoon ginger

½ teaspoon nutmeg

½ teaspoon cloves

1¼ cups heavy cream

¼ teaspoon salt

Whipped cream for serving

We use fresh pumpkin that we roast in the oven for this pie. It gives it a richer flavor than canned pumpkin.

Roll out dough for pie shell and fit into a 9-inch pie pan. Crimp the edges. Mix the remaining ingredients together until smooth. Pour into the shell and bake at 325 degrees F for about 40 minutes, or until it begins to thicken and is just a little wobbly when shaken. Serve hot or cold with lots of whipped cream sweetened with a little powdered sugar.

ROASTING PIE PUMPKINS
Start with 1 sweet pie pumpkin and cut into six wedges. Scrape out and discard the seeds and stringy stuff. Lay in the bottom of a small roasting pan. Pour in a little water. Cover the pan with foil and roast at 350 degrees F until the pumpkin is tender, about 40 minutes. When cool enough to handle, remove the skin and puree or mash the flesh. One pumpkin should yield 2 cups puree or more, depending on its size.

Pie Dough for 2 crusts
    (see recipe on page 29)
2 full pints fresh blueberries
¾ cup sugar
¼ cup cornstarch
Zest of ½ lemon
Egg wash (1 egg whisked
    with 2 tablespoons
    water)
2 tablespoons sugar

BLUEBERRY PIE

PREP TIME: 30 minutes
COOKING TIME: 45 to 60 minutes
COOLING TIME: 30 minutes
FEEDS: 6

We always make this pie when blueberries are in full season—big, fat and juicy! I would not make this pie with frozen berries, as they tend to be watery when cooked.

Roll out pie dough for bottom crust and fit into a 9-inch pie pan. Mix blueberries, sugar, cornstarch, and lemon zest in a large bowl; pour the filling into the pie shell.

Use pie dough to make a lattice top. The best technique for this is to roll out the dough in a rectangular shape. Using a pastry cutter or a small knife, cut 8 strips of dough, about 1 inch wide. Lay the two longest strips across either end, intersecting in the middle. Then weave the remaining strips outward to form a lattice top. When complete, cut the excess dough off and pinch the edges to create the border. Brush the top with egg wash and sprinkle with 2 tablespoons sugar. Bake for 45 minutes to 1 hour at 325 degrees F until done; the fruit should be bubbly and thick. Let cool for 30 minutes before serving.

BLUEBERRY PIE

PEACH COBBLER

APRICOT-BLACKBERRY CRISP

PREP TIME: 30 minutes

COOKING TIME: 40 minutes

FEEDS: 6

4 cups apricots, peeled, rinsed and sliced

2 cups blackberries

1 cup brown sugar

3 tablespoons cornstarch

2 tablespoons butter, cut into pieces

Crisp Topping (see recipe below)

Mix together apricots, blackberries, brown sugar, and cornstarch. Divide between 6 ovenproof bowls or place in a 9-inch pie pan. Break the butter into little pieces and place on top of the fruit. Use crisp topping to cover fruit, about 1 cup per bowl. Bake for 40 minutes at 325 degrees F, until fruit is bubbling and Crisp Topping is browned.

CRISP TOPPING

PREP TIME: 10 minutes

1 cup butter

2 cups brown sugar

2 cups rolled oats

3 cups flour

1½ teaspoons cinnamon

2 cups bread crumbs (optional)

The crisp topping recipe will probably make more than you need, but it will store well in the fridge for months.

Mix all ingredients together until the butter is well incorporated and the mixture is crumbly like cornmeal.

PEACH COBBLER

PREP TIME: 30 minutes

COOKING TIME: 35 minutes

FEEDS: 6

TOPPING

1 cup flour

1 teaspoon baking powder

Pinch salt

2 tablespoons butter

2 tablespoons shortening

1 egg

¼ cup buttermilk

FILLING

4 cups fresh peaches, rinsed and sliced

⅓ cup brown sugar

2 tablespoons cornstarch

Zest and juice of ½ orange

2 tablespoons sugar, for topping

The quality of the fruit makes a real difference in this dessert. Only use peaches when they are at the height of the season, juicy and flavorful. At other times of the year you can substitute apples, plums, strawberries and rhubarb, or a mix of berries.

To make the Topping: Mix flour, baking powder, and salt in the bowl of a stand mixer or a large bowl. Cut butter and shortening into small pieces and mix into flour until it becomes crumbly. Add egg and incorporate. Pour in enough buttermilk (about ¼ cup) to bring the dough together. Do not overmix or the dough will become tough.

To make the Filling: mix peaches, brown sugar, cornstarch, orange zest, and orange juice together and divide among 6 ovenproof bowls or put in a 9-inch pie pan. Break topping into little pieces and place on top of fruit. The topping should allow the juices from the fruit to cook up through it, so do not make a solid topping, but a crumbly one. Sprinkle with 2 tablespoons sugar divided among the six bowls. Cover loosely with foil and bake for 20 minutes; uncover and bake 15 minutes more. The dough should be golden brown and the fruit juice thick and bubbly.

1⅓ cups cocoa

2½ cups + 2 tablespoons
cake flour

½ tablespoon baking soda

1 cup sugar

1 cup brown sugar

½ teaspoon salt

1 cup + 2 tablespoons
butter, softened

3 eggs

3 teaspoons vanilla

3 cups buttermilk

1 recipe Fudgy Frosting
(see page 43)

1 recipe Coconut Pecan
Icing (see page 43)

German Chocolate Cake

PREP TIME: 20 minutes
COOKING TIME: 30 minutes
FEEDS: 12

Put all of the dry ingredients into the bowl of a stand mixer or a large mixing bowl. Cut butter into little pieces and mix into the dry ingredients until crumbly.

In a separate bowl, whisk together eggs, vanilla, and buttermilk. Add enough of the wet mixture to the dry mixture to make a batter. Beat on high for 2 minutes. Scrape down the sides until everything is incorporated and the batter is smooth. Turn down mixer to medium and add remaining wet ingredients in three additions, scraping the bowl after each.

Pour into two 9-inch cake pans that have been greased and fitted with a sheet of parchment paper cut to fit the bottom of the pan. Bake for approximately 30 minutes, or until a toothpick inserted in the middle of the cake comes out almost clean, with just a crumb or two clinging to it. (The sides of the cake will also be shrinking away from the pan, and the top will spring back when touched lightly.) Remove from oven and let cool to room temperature.

To assemble the cake, split the two layers in half. Frost the top of each of the four layers with Coconut Pecan Icing. Carefully stack layers on top of each other, pressing down lightly to make sure layers are set. Frost the sides of the cake with Fudgy Frosting.

Note: At sea level, increase baking soda to 4 teaspoons, decrease buttermilk to 2½ cups, and bake cakes longer, close to 1 hour.

Placing the cake layers in the refrigerator for an hour or so can make them easier to work with when you are ready to ice and fill the cake.

Fudgy Frosting

PREP TIME: 10 minutes

TURNOUT TIME: 30 minutes

4 ounces unsweetened chocolate, chopped

1 cup sugar

¾ cup evaporated milk

Melt chocolate in a double boiler over simmering water or in a glass bowl in the microwave, stopping to stir every 15 seconds. If you get the chocolate too hot you will need to let it come back to room temperature. Put the sugar and evaporated milk in a blender and mix. Then add the chocolate and mix until the frosting thickens, gets a shine on it, and is too thick to mix. Let it rest for half an hour at room temperature before frosting cake.

Coconut Pecan Icing

PREP TIME: 15 minutes

CHILLING TIME: 4 hours

1 can evaporated milk, divided

1 cup sugar

1 cup brown sugar

12 egg yolks

8 tablespoons butter

¼ teaspoon salt

5 tablespoons cornstarch

1½ teaspoons vanilla

⅔ cup toasted pecans

2 cups coconut

Put three-fourths of the can of evaporated milk, sugar, brown sugar, egg yolks, butter, and salt into a saucepan over medium-high heat. Bring to a boil while whisking.

Meanwhile, mix cornstarch in a small bowl with the remaining one-fourth can evaporated milk. Add this to the saucepan mixture and bring to a boil again. Remove from heat. Cool and add vanilla, pecans, and coconut. Cool for 4 hours or overnight.

PASTRY CREAM
2 cups milk
½ cup sugar
¼ vanilla bean
3 tablespoons cornstarch,
    sifted
¼ teaspoon salt
5 egg yolks
1 tablespoon butter

GANACHE
8 ounces semisweet
    chocolate, chopped
1 cup heavy cream

SHELLS
4 tablespoons butter
½ cup milk
½ cup water
1 cup flour
¼ teaspoon salt
3 eggs

ÉCLAIRS

PREP TIME: 45 minutes
COOKING TIME: 50 minutes
FEEDS: 14

Since we first started making éclairs, we've had a few customers who eat their éclair before their meal. Now you at least want to have your server at the Roadhouse set one aside with your name on it, because they go fast! That's why this is a larger recipe than normal. It makes fourteen éclairs, which make great gifts for teachers, friends, or yourself.

Éclairs are best eaten the day they are made. The shells don't hold up well, and the consistency changes after they are refrigerated. But the pastry cream and ganache can (and should) be made ahead of time. Then make the shells right before you want to eat—fill them, top them, and enjoy them! You'll impress everyone with these, but the real secret is that they are easy to make.

To make the Pastry Cream: Heat milk, sugar, and vanilla bean (which has been split and scraped into the milk) in a saucepan over medium heat and bring to a boil.

In a large bowl, beat cornstarch, salt, and egg yolks until fluffy and light. This is best done with an electric mixer. When the milk comes to a boil, drizzle a little into the yolks while whisking. Continue to add hot milk slowly, whisking continually until fully incorporated to protect yolks from curdling. Return saucepan to stove and whisk until mixture comes to a boil. Let it cook a little at a boil, whisking continuously. Pour through a sieve into a container; add butter and mix into the cream. Remove and reserve the ¼ vanilla bean. Cover the cream with plastic wrap

to prevent a skin from developing. Chill thoroughly for 4 hours or overnight.

VANILLA SUGAR: Always save your vanilla beans after use. Rinse them off and dry them, and then throw them in a container with some sugar to make vanilla sugar.

To make the Ganache: Put chocolate in a bowl. Bring cream to a boil in a saucepan over medium heat. Pour boiling cream over chocolate and let mixture sit for a minute; then blend until smooth. I find that ganache is smoother if it is completely chilled and then reheated to desired temperature at time of use.

To make the Shells: Bring butter, milk, and water to a boil in a saucepan. Add flour and salt all at once. Cook over medium-high heat, stirring constantly. A crust will appear on the bottom of the pan, and any flour pockets should cook out as you stir the mixture. Transfer the dough to the bowl of a stand mixer and beat with the paddle attachment on medium speed. Slow the machine down and add eggs, one at a time, beating on high after each addition. Scrape down sides as necessary to get the dough smooth. Dough should seem a little wet and shiny; if not, add another egg.

44

Put dough into a 1-gallon plastic bag or pastry bag with a ½-inch hole. On an ungreased sheet pan, squeeze out 7 thinish shells, about 1 inch in thickness and 5 inches long, from the edge to the middle of the pan. Squeeze out 7 more shells on the other side of the pan. Bake for 50 minutes at 350 degrees F, until shells are a little past golden brown and hollow inside. Remove from oven and cool for 5 to 10 minutes before assembling éclairs.

To assemble: Have Ganache warmed to room temperature (it should be warm, not hot, and able to coat the back of a spoon). Use the microwave to warm it up slowly if necessary. Cut the shells in half lengthwise and remove any extra dough from the middle. Fill the bottom half of each shell with Pastry Cream, approximately ¼ cup per shell. Dip the top half of each shell in Ganache and place on top of Pastry Cream–filled shells. Serve immediately.

FLOURLESS CHOCOLATE CAKE

PREP TIME: 20 minutes

COOKING TIME: 30 minutes

FEEDS: 10

1 pound bittersweet
    chocolate, chopped
1 cup butter
9 eggs, separated
¾ cup + 1 tablespoon sugar
Powdered sugar for dusting

This is an easy yet elegant dessert. It goes great with fresh berries and whipped cream.

Melt the chocolate and butter together in a double boiler. Set aside to cool. Beat egg yolks with ¾ cup sugar at high speed until batter falls in ribbons. In a separate bowl, beat egg whites until they start to turn white and foamy; then add 1 tablespoon sugar and continue beating until stiff but not dry. Fold chocolate into the egg yolk batter. Then, in three additions, carefully fold in egg whites.

Bake in a 10-inch springform pan that has been greased and lined with parchment paper. Bake at 325 degrees F for 30 minutes, until firm on top but still jiggly in the middle. Let cool to room temperature. Dust with powdered sugar and serve slices with whipped cream.

HOW TO MAKE GREAT PANCAKES 48

STRAWBERRY-LEMON RICOTTA CAKES 48

BLUEBERRY BUCKWHEAT CAKES 50

BUTTERMILK PANCAKES 50

HOW TO MAKE GREAT WAFFLES 51

LEMON POPPY SEED WAFFLES 51

BLUE CORNMEAL WAFFLES 52

PUMPKIN WAFFLES 52

CHOCOLATE FRENCH TOAST 54

FEATHER-LIGHT CORNMEAL MUFFINS 54

COFFEE CAKE 55

PUMPKIN MUFFINS 57

CINNAMON-SUGAR MUFFINS 57

ROADHOUSE GRANOLA 58

BLUEBERRY OR CRANBERRY MUFFINS 58

MOCHA WALNUT MUFFINS 59

BISCUITS 59

CINNAMON ROLLS 61

SMOKED TURKEY, SWEET POTATO,

AND ANDOUILLE HASH 62

RED FLANNEL HASH 62

HUEVOS MOTULEÑOS 64

BREAKFAST BURRITO 64

MIGAS 67

HUEVOS DIVORCIADOS 67 ·

CHILE RELLENOS OMELET 68

COUNTRY GRAVY 68

HUEVOS EN BRODO 69

GREEN EGGS AND HAM 70

PAN-FRIED TROUT AND EGGS

WITH BACON 70

RED-EYE GRAVY WITH BISCUITS

AND HAM 71

HOW TO MAKE GREAT PANCAKES There are a few simple rules to follow to ensure that you will have excellent pancakes every time. Always mix the dry ingredients first. Mix wet ingredients separately and then fold into the dry. Do not overmix the batter or your pancakes will be tough. Mix until the ingredients are just barely combined. Heat a cast-iron pan on high, then reduce heat to medium-high. Put 2 tablespoons of butter into the hot pan and melt it, coating the pan. Ladle the pancake batter into the pan, about ½ cup for each cake, unless otherwise stated. Resist flipping the cakes until bubbles form on the top. Flip the cakes and cook 1 to 1½ minutes more until pancakes are set.

STRAWBERRY-LEMON RICOTTA CAKES

PREP TIME: **20 minutes**

TURNOUT TIME: **5 to 10 minutes**

FEEDS: **4**

2 cups flour
2 teaspoons baking powder
1 teaspoon baking soda
¼ teaspoon salt
¼ cup sugar
⅓ cup butter, melted
1 cup whole-milk ricotta
1½ cups milk
2 eggs, separated
Zest of 2 lemons
Powdered sugar to garnish
Butter for spreading
1 pint strawberries, sliced
Maple syrup

Mix dry ingredients together in a large bowl. In another bowl, whisk together melted butter, ricotta, milk, egg yolks, and lemon zest. Combine the wet ingredients with the dry ingredients.

Meanwhile, beat egg whites until they hold a soft peak. Fold them into the batter.

Cook as described in the sidebar "How to Make Great Pancakes" on this page, but use only ¼ cup batter for each cake. These cakes may take a little extra time to cook. Test one to make sure it is cooked through before removing from pan. Dust the finished cakes with powdered sugar and serve with butter, sliced strawberries, and maple syrup.

The ricotta cakes are a great special-occasion breakfast and a real showstopper. The ricotta packs them with protein so they leave you feeling fueled for the day.

STRAWBERRY-LEMON RICOTTA CAKES

BLUEBERRY BUCKWHEAT CAKES

PREP TIME: 10 minutes

TURNOUT TIME: 5 to 10 minutes

FEEDS: 4

1 cup white flour
1 cup buckwheat flour
¼ cup sugar
2 teaspoons baking powder
1 teaspoon baking soda
½ teaspoon salt
2 eggs
2 cups buttermilk
¼ cup butter, melted
1 pint blueberries
2 tablespoons butter,
  for pan
Blueberries for garnish
Maple syrup
Butter for spreading

Prepare and cook as described in "How to Make Great Pancakes" on page 48. Drop blueberries into the batter of each cake as you ladle them onto the pan.

Serve with more fresh blueberries, real maple syrup, and butter.

This is a good basic recipe that can be used for many variations. We make whole wheat cakes and yellow cornmeal–lemon cakes using this recipe. For whole wheat cakes, just replace the buckwheat flour with whole wheat flour. For cornmeal–lemon cakes, replace buckwheat flour with cornmeal and add the zest of 1 lemon. If you want to use milk instead of buttermilk in this recipe, reduce to 1½ cups.

BUTTERMILK PANCAKES

PREP TIME: 5 minutes

TURNOUT TIME: 5 to 10 minutes

FEEDS: 4

3 cups flour
3 teaspoons baking soda*
1½ teaspoons salt
4 cups buttermilk
4 eggs
¾ cup butter, melted

*Add ½ teaspoon more baking soda at sea level.

Mix dry ingredients together in a large bowl. In another bowl, whisk together wet ingredients. Combine the wet ingredients with the dry ingredients. Cook as described in "How to Make Great Pancakes" on page 48.

Serve with maple syrup, butter, and any fruit in season, or just plain.

Kids like these pancakes with chocolate chips dropped into the cakes on the griddle. If you add banana slices and more chocolate chips sprinkled on top, you'll be the best cook ever.

HOW TO MAKE GREAT WAFFLES As with pancake batter, overmixing is a no-no. Mix together dry ingredients and wet ingredients separately. Then combine until mixed, but do not overmix. Follow your waffle iron manufacturer's directions on how to cook them. The batters in this cookbook will hold up for a couple of days, so if you make waffles for Sunday brunch, you can cook up the leftovers Monday morning in a jiffy!

LEMON POPPY SEED WAFFLES

PREP TIME: **10** minutes

TURNOUT TIME: **5 to 10** minutes

FEEDS: **4**

2 cups flour
½ teaspoon salt
1 tablespoon baking
    powder
½ teaspoon baking soda
¼ cup sugar
1½ tablespoons poppy seeds
3 lemons, zested
¼ cup butter, melted
1⅔ cups milk
1 tablespoon vanilla
4 eggs
1 teaspoon lemon extract

These waffles are light, zesty, and not too sweet. They go perfectly with fresh berries, a citrus butter, or whipped cream.

Mix together the dry ingredients. Zest lemons without getting into the white, bitter pith. Mix the lemon zest together with the wet ingredients and fold into the dry ingredients until incorporated. Cook according to directions for "How to Make Great Waffles" on this page.

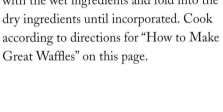

BLUE CORNMEAL WAFFLES

PREP TIME: 5 minutes

TURNOUT TIME: 5 to 10 minutes

FEEDS: 6

1½ cups blue cornmeal
1½ cups flour
½ tablespoon baking
    powder
½ teaspoon baking soda
½ teaspoon salt
¼ cup sugar
2 cups buttermilk
4 eggs
⅓ cup butter, melted

To make the batter, follow the directions for "How to Make Great Waffles" on page 51. We serve this waffle with honey butter and sliced bananas. But there are many possibilities, including sliced strawberries.

The texture of the blue cornmeal holds up well against sauces and syrups. Makes 6 waffles.

PUMPKIN WAFFLES

PREP TIME: 5 minutes

TURNOUT TIME: 5 to 10 minutes

FEEDS: 6

3 cups flour
5 teaspoons baking powder
2 teaspoons cinnamon
1 teaspoon allspice
1 teaspoon ginger
1 teaspoon salt
⅓ cup brown sugar
3 tablespoons maple syrup
1⅓ cups pumpkin puree
2¼ cups milk
5 eggs
⅓ cup butter, melted

To make the batter, follow the directions for "How to Make Great Waffles" on page 51. This is a soufflé-like waffle that tastes like pumpkin pie. It's great on a cold fall morning. We usually serve it with orange butter and toasted pecans.

Another great variation is to use sweet potato puree. If you use sweet potato puree, eliminate the allspice and use only half the cinnamon. Substitute ½ cup orange juice for ½ cup of the milk, and add the zest of 1 orange.

ORANGE BUTTER
½ cup butter, softened
¼ cup powdered sugar
½ teaspoon orange extract
Zest of ½ orange

Beat the butter with the sugar until smooth. Add the extract and zest. Save any extra butter for another day.

BLUE CORNMEAL WAFFLES

CHOCOLATE FRENCH TOAST

PREP TIME: 10 minutes

TURNOUT TIME: 5 to 10 minutes

FEEDS: 4

1 cup milk

½ cup sugar

1 cup half-and-half

½ cup chopped semisweet chocolate

4 eggs

½ teaspoon vanilla

1 teaspoon almond extract

½ loaf sourdough bread, cut in 1-inch slices

This is a decadent variation on plain old French toast.

Put milk into a saucepan with sugar and half-and-half; scald. Remove from heat and add chocolate.

Meanwhile, whisk together eggs, vanilla, and almond extract in a mixing bowl.

Whisk the hot milk mixture to a smooth consistency, then slowly whisk this mix into the eggs until smooth. Soak bread slices in the batter, one at a time, squeezing them to help the bread absorb the batter. Cook the slices on a buttered griddle or cast-iron pan at medium heat. Let the toast brown and get slightly crusty, then flip and cook until a light crust forms on the other side. Push on the bread with your finger to see if it is cooked through.

Serve hot with whipped cream, toasted almonds, and syrup. Fresh raspberries also make a nice touch.

FEATHER-LIGHT CORNMEAL MUFFINS

PREP TIME: 10 minutes

COOKING TIME: 30 minutes

FEEDS: 6

2 cups flour

1 cup cornmeal

½ cup sugar

2 teaspoons baking powder*

½ teaspoon salt

4 eggs

⅔ cup milk

½ cup butter, melted

1 cup berries, dried fruit, or nuts

This is a good, basic muffin batter to use with fresh berries in the summer or cranberries or dried fruit in the winter. The crunch of the cornmeal gives these muffins a great texture.

Mix together dry ingredients in a large bowl. In another bowl, whisk together wet ingredients. Combine the wet with the dry ingredients. Fold in fruit or nuts of choice. Bake in a greased muffin tin at 325 degrees F for 30 minutes, or until a tester comes out clean.

*At sea level, add an additional 1 teaspoon of baking powder and bake 10 minutes longer, or until tester comes out clean.

COFFEE CAKE

PREP TIME: 15 minutes
COOKING TIME: 45 minutes
FEEDS: 8 (generous portions)

To make the Filling: Place all ingredients, walnuts first, in a food processor and process to a crumbly texture. Set aside while making batter.

To make the Batter: Sift together flour, baking powder, baking soda, and salt in a large bowl. Cream butter and sugar in the bowl of a stand mixer using a paddle attachment. When the mixture is light and fluffy, add vanilla and eggs, one at a time, scraping down sides as needed. When well creamed and fluffy, add the sifted dry ingredients alternately with sour cream. Be careful not to overmix. (Overmixing batter leads to tough cakes.)

Grease and flour a 12-cup Bundt pan or spray with nonstick cooking spray. Place a third of the batter in bottom of pan. Place half of filling over the top of the batter. Repeat layers, adding another layer of batter, then rest of filling, and ending with the final layer of batter on top. Bake for 45 minutes, or until cake tester comes out dry. Serve warm, with butter if you dare!

This coffee cake is based on Maeda Haetter's famous recipe. We've had it on the menu at Harry's since we first opened the restaurant. It is rich and buttery. The filling gives it the crunch of nuts and the sweet aroma of cinnamon and brown sugar.

FILLING
1 cup walnuts
1 cup brown sugar
1 tablespoon cinnamon
1 tablespoon cocoa

BATTER
3 cups flour
½ tablespoon baking powder
½ tablespoon baking soda
½ teaspoon salt
¾ cup butter
1½ cups sugar
3 teaspoons vanilla
3 eggs
2 cups sour cream

CINNAMON-SUGAR MUFFINS

PUMPKIN MUFFINS

PREP TIME: 10 minutes

COOKING TIME: 30 minutes

FEEDS: 8

These muffins are wonderfully soufflé-like. They're perfect on a brisk fall morning. You can add 1 cup chopped nuts for a little texture if you like.

Mix dry ingredients together in a large bowl. In another bowl, whisk together wet ingredients. Add wet ingredients to the dry ingredients and stir until smooth.

Spoon batter into greased muffin tins and bake at 325 degrees F for 30 minutes, or until a tester comes out clean. Makes 8 large or 16 small muffins.

We also make these muffins with sweet potato puree. If you do, add only the cinnamon and the zest of 1 orange for seasoning.

*At sea level, add 1¾ teaspoons more of baking powder and bake until tester comes out clean.

4½ cups flour

1 teaspoon salt

1 tablespoon baking powder*

1½ teaspoons cinnamon

1½ teaspoons nutmeg

1½ teaspoons allspice

1 cup butter, melted

2 cups brown sugar

½ cup maple syrup

2 cups milk

6 eggs

2 cups pumpkin puree

CINNAMON-SUGAR MUFFINS

PREP TIME: 10 minutes

COOKING TIME: 30 minutes

FEEDS: 6

To make the Batter: Cream butter and shortening with sugar in the bowl of a stand mixer until fluffy. Add eggs, one at a time.

Mix together dry ingredients. Add alternately with milk. Spoon batter into a greased muffin tin and bake at 325 degrees F for 30 minutes, or until a tester comes out clean.

For the Topping: Brush muffins with melted butter and roll in cinnamon-sugar. Makes 6 large or 12 small muffins.

*At sea level, add an additional 1¾ teaspoons of baking powder and bake for an additional 10 minutes, or until tester comes out clean.

BATTER

¾ cup butter

6 tablespoons shortening

⅔ cup sugar

2 eggs

1 teaspoon salt

2½ teaspoons baking powder*

½ teaspoon nutmeg

3 cups flour

1 cup milk

TOPPING

1 cup butter, melted

1 cup sugar mixed with 1½ tablespoons cinnamon

ROADHOUSE GRANOLA

PREP TIME: 10 minutes

COOKING TIME: 20 minutes

FEEDS: 8

4 cups rolled oats

1 cup sliced almonds

1 cup coconut

2 teaspoons cinnamon

1 teaspoon nutmeg

1 teaspoon vanilla

1 cup apple juice

½ cup maple syrup

½ cup dried cranberries, raisins, or other dried fruit

Some people have been known to travel to foreign countries with a stash of Roadhouse Granola in their suitcase! It is pretty addictive, and it's good for you. It's great with fruit and yogurt, on top of pancakes and waffles, or as a snack straight out of the bag.

Mix oats, almonds, coconut, cinnamon, and nutmeg together in a bowl. Add vanilla, apple juice, and maple syrup. Spread on a greased sheet pan and bake at 350 degrees F for 10 minutes. Then mix and bake 10 minutes more. Mix frequently and keep baking until all is crunchy and golden brown. Remove from oven and cool. Then add the cranberries or raisins. Store in a tightly covered container.

BLUEBERRY OR CRANBERRY MUFFINS

PREP TIME: 10 minutes

COOKING TIME: 30 minutes

FEEDS: 6

1½ teaspoons baking powder*

½ teaspoon salt

2½ cups flour

½ cup butter, softened

½ cup sugar

½ cup brown sugar

3 eggs

1 cup milk

Zest of ½ lemon

1 teaspoon lemon extract

½ pint blueberries or cranberries

*At sea level, add an additional 1½ teaspoons of baking powder and bake an additional 10 minutes, or until tester comes out clean.

This batter makes a cake-like muffin. It is good with fresh berries.

Mix the dry ingredients together in a large bowl and set aside. Cream butter, sugar, and brown sugar in the bowl of a stand mixer or with an electric mixer until light and fluffy. Add eggs, one at a time. The batter will seem a little broken at this point, but it will come together. Add dry ingredients to the wet ingredients alternately with milk—three additions of dry and two of milk. By hand, fold in the lemon zest, lemon extract, and berries. Spoon batter into a greased muffin tin and bake at 325 degrees F for 30 minutes, or until a tester comes out clean. Makes 6 large or 12 small muffins.

For a great variation, eliminate the berries and add 2 tablespoons poppy seeds and zest of 1 additional lemon.

Mocha Walnut Muffins

PREP TIME: 10 minutes

TURNOUT TIME: 30 minutes

FEEDS: 6

1/3 cup+ 1 tablespoon butter

1/3 cup sugar

1/3 cup brown sugar

2 teaspoons vanilla

3 tablespoons instant coffee

2 eggs

2 1/4 cups flour

1/4 teaspoon salt

1 1/2 teaspoons baking powder*

2/3 cup milk

3/4 cup chopped semisweet chocolate

3/4 cup walnuts

These muffins are like a dessert. They have gained a real following at breakfast, but also make a satisfying mid-afternoon pick-me-up.

Cream butter and sugars in the bowl of a stand mixer. Add vanilla and instant coffee. Then add eggs, one at a time.

Mix the dry ingredients together and add to the wet ingredients alternately with milk. Fold in chocolate and walnuts at the last. Spoon batter into a greased muffin tin and bake at 325 degrees F for 30 minutes, or until a tester comes out clean. Makes 6 large or 12 small muffins.

At sea level, add an additional 1 teaspoon of baking powder and bake for an additional 10 minutes, or until tester comes out clean.

Biscuits

PREP TIME: 10 minutes

TURNOUT TIME: 30 minutes

FEEDS: 6

2 cups flour

1 tablespoon sugar

2 teaspoons baking powder*

1/2 teaspoon salt

5 tablespoons cold butter, cut into small pieces

3/4 cup buttermilk

Mix dry ingredients in the bowl of a stand mixer with a paddle attachment. Cut in butter until the mix is crumbly. Add just enough buttermilk to bring the mix together as a dough. It should not be too wet. Do not overmix or the dough will be tough.

Roll out dough on a floured board and cut out biscuits. Place on a greased or nonstick sheet pan and bake at 350 degrees F for 30 minutes, or until golden brown on top. Makes 6 large or 12 small biscuits.

We serve these biscuits with Red-Eye Gravy and Country Gravy (see pages 71 and 68) at breakfast and Fried Chicken (see page 133) at dinner. But they are good anytime with a little butter and honey. We also use this dough to make Tomato Corn Biscuit Pie (see page 139).

At sea level, add an additional 1 teaspoon of baking powder and bake an additional 10 minutes, or until tester comes out dry.

CINNAMON ROLL PRODUCTION

Cinnamon Rolls

PREP TIME: 10 minutes to make dough; 10 minutes to assemble rolls
TURNOUT TIME: 8 hours plus 1½ hours
FEEDS: 6

This recipe makes 6 large cinnamon rolls and can easily be doubled. In a large bowl, mix yeast in water. The water should be lukewarm (about 100 degrees F), not hot, or it could kill the yeast. Mix in ½ tablespoon sugar and set bowl in a warm place. If your yeast is good, the mixture will foam up in a few minutes. If not, get some fresh yeast and start over.

To make the Dough: Put flour, salt, and ½ cup sugar in the bowl of a stand mixer. Turn on low until ingredients are just combined. Cut butter into little pieces and add to dry ingredients. Turn the mixer motor on low and let butter incorporate until the mixture is crumbly. Add egg yolks, then the risen yeast mixture, and finally the milk. These additions should happen quickly so the dough does not become too wet for the milk to be incorporated well. Put dough in a large plastic container with room to grow, and cover with plastic wrap. Refrigerate 8 hours or overnight.

To assemble rolls: Roll dough into a rectangle about 20 by 30 inches. Brush with a thin layer of melted butter. Sprinkle with brown sugar, cinnamon, and chopped pecans. Roll up the dough starting on the short side to create a log. With your hands, shape the log into an evenly thick roll and cut into 6 equal pieces. Grease the muffin tin cups and place each slice into a cup. Put in a warm place to rise. This usually takes about 45 minutes to an hour, depending on how warm the spot is. The dough will be soft and a little spongy when ready to bake.

Cover the rolls with foil and bake for 20 minutes at 350 degrees F. Then uncover and bake for 15 minutes more, until the rolls are golden brown all over. Flip the tin upside down and the cinnamon rolls will come right out. Let sit for a couple of minutes and then invert the rolls and serve warm with butter. Ahhhh!

This is the recipe that makes me feel like a magician. It is not that difficult, but it takes planning: you need to make the dough a day ahead. But when these beauties come out of the oven, it's all worth it. We serve cinnamon rolls on Saturday and Sunday mornings only. It's one of the rituals I love about the restaurant. Because they take a while to rise, the rolls usually don't come out of the oven until close to 8:00 a.m. The counter at Harry's is usually packed by this time, and all the customers "ooh" and "aah."

That makes it worth getting out of bed at 5:30 a.m. on a weekend morning!

DOUGH

1 tablespoon active dry yeast
¼ cup warm water
½ tablespoon sugar
3½ cups flour
1 teaspoon salt
½ cup sugar
1 cup butter
3 egg yolks
1¼ cups milk

FILLING

¼ cup butter, melted
2 cups brown sugar
3 tablespoons cinnamon
1 cup chopped pecans

SMOKED TURKEY, SWEET POTATO, AND ANDOUILLE HASH

PREP TIME: 30 minutes

TURNOUT TIME: 10 minutes

FEEDS: 8

3 pounds diced smoked turkey

6 cups peeled and diced sweet potatoes

1 cup diced yellow onion

1 cup diced red bell peppers

1 cup diced poblano chiles

10 ounces diced Andouille sausage

3 tablespoons butter

¾ teaspoon salt

¼ teaspoon pepper

¼ teaspoon or less cayenne

¼ teaspoon oregano

¼ cup chicken stock

¼ cup heavy cream

8 poached eggs

Chop turkey, sweet potatoes, onion, bell pepper, chiles, and sausage into ¼-inch dice. Parboil sweet potatoes in a pot of boiling salted water for 5 to 10 minutes. Do not overcook; they will go from very hard to mush quickly. The potatoes should have some bite. Drain and cool.

In a cast-iron skillet sauté the onion, bell pepper, and chiles until they start to soften.

Add sausage and cook for about 5 minutes, until it starts to brown; then add turkey and seasonings. Cook for another 5 minutes, then add sweet potatoes, stock, and cream. Stir and scrape bottom of skillet. When the liquids are absorbed, the hash is ready. Spoon into bowls and top with poached eggs.

RED FLANNEL HASH

PREP TIME: 1 hour

TURNOUT TIME: 10 minutes

FEEDS: 4

1 cup diced onions

1 cup diced cooked carrots

1 cup diced turnips and/or parsnips (optional)

1 cup diced cooked beets

2½ cups diced cooked potatoes

4 cups diced corned beef

2 tablespoons butter

1 tablespoon salt

¼ teaspoon pepper

¼ teaspoon thyme

½ cup heavy cream

4 poached eggs

This is one of our more colorful dishes. Traditionally, it is a snack made from leftovers from a New England boiled dinner. We love to add turnips and/or parsnips to the mix, but they are optional.

Dice vegetables and corned beef into ¼-inch dice. Blanch all of the vegetables except onions separately in salted water until tender but still firm.

Heat a cast-iron pan. Add butter and sauté onion until soft. Add corned beef and cook for a few minutes, and then add vegetables and seasoning. Cook for a few minutes more and then fold in cream. Cook for 2 or 3 minutes more and taste for seasoning. Top with poached eggs and serve.

RED FLANNEL HASH

SALSA

½ habanero chile*
5 tomatoes
½ onion, diced
5 cloves garlic
2 tablespoons orange juice
1 teaspoon Mexican oregano
¼ teaspoon cumin
¼ teaspoon anise
1 cup stock (chicken or
   vegetable)
1 tablespoon vegetable oil
2 teaspoons salt
¼ teaspoon black pepper

TOPPING

8 corn tortillas
1 cup Refritos Negros
   (see page 147)
8 eggs, fried any style
½ cup frozen peas, thawed
1 cup diced ham
½ cup crumbled feta cheese
Ripe plantains or bananas,
   sliced and fried

HUEVOS MOTULEÑOS

PREP TIME: 30 minutes

TURNOUT TIME: 10 minutes

FEEDS: 4

To make the Salsa: Set habanero aside. Char tomatoes, onion, and garlic in a heavy skillet. Combine with orange juice, oregano, cumin, anise, stock, oil, salt, and pepper and blend. Cut a slit in the bottom of the habanero, and then place it in the salsa and let sit overnight or for a minimum of 2 hours. In the Yucatan there is a saying, "Let the chile take a walk through the sauce." Before serving, remove and discard the chile.

Fry tortillas in a little vegetable oil until they start to get crispy.

To serve: Place 1 tortilla on each of four plates. Spread with a thin layer of Refried Black Beans. Top with a little salsa, a second tortilla, eggs, more salsa, and then peas, ham, and feta. Garnish with fried slices of plantain or banana.

You may substitute habanero hot sauce to taste rather than using the actual chile.

---

4 large red potatoes (½ cup
   sliced per burrito)
8 slices bacon, cooked
8 to 12 eggs
Butter to coat pan
4 (8-inch) flour tortillas
2 cups Red Chile or Green
   Chile, (see recipes on
   pages 148 and 150)
1⅓ cups grated cheese
   (⅓ cup per burrito)
4 pickled jalapeños

BREAKFAST BURRITO

PREP TIME: with Green Chile, 30 minutes; with Red Chile, 1 hour

TURNOUT TIME: 5 to 10 minutes

FEEDS: 4

Preheat oven to 350 degrees F. Boil potatoes until soft in enough salted water to cover. Let cool and slice in half, and then into ¼-inch pieces.

Meanwhile, cook bacon in a skillet until crispy. Brown the potatoes in a pan with a little oil. Scramble eggs. When they start to set, fold in hot potatoes. Divide into four

portions. Place each portion into an 8-inch flour tortilla, top with bacon, and roll up.

Place burritos on an oven-safe serving dish. Top each burrito with heated chile and cheese; melt cheese by placing dish in oven for about 2 to 3 minutes. Serve with a pickled jalapeño or your choice of garnishes.

MIGAS

Migas

PREP TIME: 20 minutes

TURNOUT TIME: 5 minutes

FEEDS: 4

2 cups tortilla strips or high-quality tortilla chips

8 eggs

½ onion, diced (about ½ cup)

½ green bell pepper, diced (about ½ cup)

4 tablespoons butter

¾ cup chorizo (optional)

1 large tomato, diced

4 tablespoons diced pickled jalapeño

Salt and pepper to taste

Make the tortilla strips according to directions on page 16. You may substitute high-quality tortilla chips for this step.

Crack the eggs in a large bowl and whisk. Set aside. In a large sauté pan, cook onion and bell pepper in butter, leaving some crunch to the vegetables. Remove vegetables. In the same pan, cook the chorizo through. Add tomato and pickled jalapeños. When they are heated through, return the sauteéd vegetables to the pan and add the whisked eggs. Cook over medium heat until the eggs are about half set, then add tortilla strips. Season with salt and pepper. The tortilla strips should still have some crunch to them when the dish is served.

Serve with beans and a flour tortilla, and top with grated cheese.

Huevos Divorciados

PREP TIME: 30 minutes for salsa

TURNOUT TIME: 20 minutes

FEEDS: 4

8 medium to large shrimp

2½ cups Tomatillo Salsa (see page 146)

8 corn tortillas

2 cups Refritos Negros (see page 147)

2½ cups Salsa Cascabel (see page 146)

8 eggs

½ cup feta cheese or queso fresco

½ cup Cotija cheese

2 tablespoons chopped cilantro, for garnish

I first had these in Mexico City. They are like huevos rancheros, but the two eggs are divided in half, separated in the center by refried black beans. This is our version, but the variations are endless. In place of Tomatillo Salsa or Salsa Cascabel, this dish can be made with any leftover salsas you may have.

Poach shrimp in Tomatillo Salsa until cooked through.

Wet tortillas and steam them in a hot sauté pan for 20 to 30 seconds, or until they start to soften and become pliable. Place 2 tortillas each on opposite sides of four large plates, and place Refried Black Beans in the center of each plate, between the tortillas. Heat your two salsas, using a pan or a microwave. Cover 1 tortilla with a little Salsa Cascabel and the other tortilla with a little Tomatillo Salsa.

Cook your eggs any style, and divide into 8 portions. Place one portion on each of the 8 tortillas. Top each egg with a little more of the same salsa used for each tortilla.

Place cooked shrimp on the tortilla with Tomatillo Salsa and top with feta cheese. Top the tortilla with Salsa Cascabel with grated Cotija. Garnish with chopped cilantro and serve.

 **Make salsas and beans ahead of time.**

ROASTED TOMATO SALSA

4 green chiles (poblano or
    fresh Hatch), roasted
    and peeled
1 ear roasted corn (or
    substitute 1½ cups frozen
    corn)
4 tomatoes
½ onion
1 clove garlic
2 tablespoons chopped
    cilantro
½ stick toasted and ground
    canela or substitute
    1½ teaspoon ground
    cinnamon
¾ teaspoon salt
Pinch pepper
¼ cup vegetable stock

OMELET

3 to 4 tablespoons butter
12 eggs
2 cups Asadero cheese

CHILE RELLENOS OMELET

PREP TIME: 30 minutes for sauce
TURNOUT TIME: 5 to 10 minutes
FEEDS: 4

To make the Roasted Tomato Salsa: Roast chiles according to directions on page 16 and set aside. Roast corn according to directions on page 16 and set aside. Roast tomatoes, onion, and garlic according to directions on page 16; let cool. Once cool, process roasted ingredients (except chiles and corn) along with all remaining ingredients in a food processor. You want a little texture, so do not overprocess. Fold in corn at the end. Taste for seasoning.

To make the Omelet: Coat omelet pan with butter. Crack 3 eggs in a bowl and whisk. When butter starts to foam, pour eggs into pan. Cook until omelet is halfway set. Place 1 whole roasted chile on top, spread out flat, so that the skin side of the chile is facing up, covering as much surface area as possible. Flip omelet completely over and top with cheese. Let cheese melt and then fold omelet. The green chile should now be on the outside. Repeat for remaining three omelets. Top each with warm Roasted Tomato Salsa and serve.

6 cups milk
1½ cups diced onion
4 tablespoons butter
    (or bacon fat)
3 ounces breakfast sausage
    (we use turkey sausage)
½ cup flour
1½ teaspoon salt
¼ teaspoon coarse ground
    pepper
½ teaspoon mild chile
    powder

COUNTRY GRAVY

PREP TIME: 30 minutes

In a pot, heat milk to scalding. In a second pot, sauté diced onions in butter until they are clear. Remove sausage from casing. Add sausage. As it cooks, mash with a potato masher so the meat crumbles into little pieces. When the meat is cooked through, add flour and stir to make a roux. Cook over low heat for about five minutes. Whisk in hot milk, bring to a boil and turn down heat. Add all the seasonings. Liquid should slowly bubble. Be sure to scrape the bottom of the pot with a spoon, as the gravy will tend to burn on the bottom. Simmer for about 15 minutes. Turn down heat and taste for salt and pepper. Serve over biscuits.

HUEVOS EN BRODO

PREP TIME: 30 minutes

TURNOUT TIME: 5 to 10 minutes

FEEDS: 4

To make the Sauce: Roast tomatoes, onion, and garlic according to directions on page 16. Roast and peel chiles. Cut one chile into long, thin strips and reserve for garnish. If using fresh corn, roast in husk at 350 degrees F for 25 minutes and then cut off the kernels to make 1 cup. If using frozen corn kernels, bake for 15 minutes at 325 degrees F on a sheet pan with a little oil.

In a food processor, combine cilantro, roasted tomatoes, onion, garlic, and chiles and pulse until chunky. Season with ground canela, salt, and pepper; add enough stock to make it thin enough for poaching eggs. (Remember, when you bring the liquid to a boil it will tend to thicken.) Add black beans.

Cut cheese into pieces about ¼ inch thick. Cook them in a hot, dry pan until they melt and become brown. Set aside.

All of the prep work up to this point should be done ahead. You may even do it the night before.

Heat sauce in a 10-inch sauté pan; when liquid comes to a boil, add eggs. They will poach in the liquid. While they are cooking, baste with broth from the pan. Heat the cheese. When the eggs are poached to the desired doneness, place the cheese in the bottom of serving bowls, top with sauce and eggs, and garnish with fried tortilla strips and poblano strips.

Mozzarella or Monterey Jack can be substituted.

SAUCE

5 tomatoes
½ yellow onion
1 whole garlic clove
2 poblano chiles
1 cup corn
2 tablespoons chopped cilantro leaves
2 tablespoons ground canela
Salt and pepper to taste
3 to 4 cups vegetable stock
1 cup black beans, rinsed and drained
½ pound Queso Oaxaqueño* or Panela cheese, cut in ¼-inch slices
8 eggs

GARNISH

2 tortillas, cut into strips (see page 16) or high-quality tortilla chips
Reserved chile strips

8 fresh roasted green chiles,
   hot or mild
4 slices ham
Butter
8 slices favorite breakfast
   bread
1½ cups sharp cheddar
   cheese
8 eggs

Harry I am, and
I love green eggs
and ham!

GREEN EGGS AND HAM

TURNOUT TIME: 10 minutes

FEEDS: 4

Inspired by Dr. Seuss, this could be the best breakfast sandwich ever!

Roast, peel, seed, and devein chiles as described on page 16. On a griddle, heat up ham. Butter bread and place butter-side-down on a cast-iron pan. Put one slice of heated ham on each of four slices of bread. On the other four slices, place some of the cheese and green chiles.

In a skillet, crack eggs. Cook eggs as for over easy, but just before flipping them poke the yolks, then flip. (You want the yolks to be almost set or the sandwich will be too runny. But you do not want it to get too dry.) Place 2 cooked eggs on each ham slice. Then place the slices of bread with chiles and cheese on top of the slices of bread with ham and eggs to make sandwiches. Cut and serve. Make sure that the cheese has melted.

4 trout fillets
1 cup cornmeal, seasoned
   with 1 teaspoon salt and a
   pinch of pepper
Vegetable oil for frying
8 slices bacon
8 eggs

PAN-FRIED TROUT AND EGGS WITH BACON

PREP TIME: 10 minutes

TURNOUT TIME: 10 minutes

FEEDS: 4

Serve this dish with home fries or hash brown potatoes.

Trim the head, collar bone, and any hard fins from the trout. Press into seasoned cornmeal; turn over and press other side into cornmeal. Heat oil in a sauté pan and cook trout until done, about two minutes on each side. Cook bacon until crisp. Cook eggs any way you like.

Red-Eye Gravy with Biscuits and Ham

PREP TIME: 30 minutes

TURNOUT TIME: 10 minutes

FEEDS: 4

If serving for breakfast, you can make the Red-Eye the day before.

To make the Seasoning Mix: Combine ingredients in a small bowl and set aside.

To make the Gravy: Fry bacon in butter. When bacon is cooked but not crunchy, add Seasoning Mix and cook for about 30 seconds. Add flour to make a roux. Cook over low heat until flour gets a nutty smell, and then add heated coffee and stock. Let the mixture come to a boil; turn down and simmer for 2 to 3 minutes. Stir in cream and brown sugar. Cook for about 5 minutes more. Yields 6 cups.

Spoon over Biscuits and ham. If you can get your hands on real country ham, this dish will become really special. Serve with eggs cooked any style.

> Preparing Red-Eye Gravy and Country Gravy are like cooking up a piece of our heritage. Nothing goes better with biscuits. This is my favorite cure for a hangover.

> Why is it called red-eye? Is it the color of truckers' eyes? The color of your eyes after all of that coffee? The reddish color from the ham and the coffee? You decide.

SEASONING MIX
2 teaspoons paprika
½ teaspoon dry mustard
1 teaspoon garlic powder
1 teaspoon onion powder
½ teaspoon white pepper
½ teaspoon thyme
½ teaspoon allspice

GRAVY
5 slices bacon, diced
¼ cup butter
⅓ cup flour
3 cups coffee, heated
2 cups stock, heated
½ cup cream
1 teaspoon salt
2 tablespoons brown sugar

1 recipe Biscuits (see page 59)
4 slices ham, heated in frying pan

SMOKED DUCK FLAUTAS WITH MANGO SAUCE 74

INDIAN SHRIMP FRITTERS 77

QUESO FUNDIDO WITH VEGGIES 78

QUESO FUNDIDO WITH MUSHROOMS 78

POLENTA CAKES WITH SMOKED DUCK AND WILD RICE 79

STUFFED SQUASH BLOSSOMS 80

BAYOU-SPICED SHRIMP 80

SHRIMP AND GRITS 81

MULLIGATAWNY 82

SOPA DE LIMA 82

CHILE CORN CHOWDER 83

SMOKED DUCK FLAUTAS WITH MANGO SAUCE

PREP TIME: 4 hours

TURNOUT TIME: 10 minutes

FEEDS: 8

SMOKED DUCK

Salt and pepper to taste

4 legs or 1 whole duck

2 tablespoons mild chile
   powder

FLAUTAS

1 tablespoon cilantro

2 green onions

2 tablespoons Mango Sauce
   (see recipe on page 150)

1 teaspoon salt

Pinch pepper

16 corn tortillas

Oil for frying

Mango Sauce for serving

Smoke the duck and make the flautas ahead of time. If you cannot smoke the duck it may be slow-roasted in the oven. Flautas may be rolled in advance, although preferably on the day they are cooked. Fry just before serving.

To make the Smoked Duck: Salt and pepper the duck and rub with chile powder. The duck may be smoked in a Weber-type grill. Light the charcoal and when the coals turn white, place them to one side. Add apple or hickory wood chips soaked in water to the coals just before starting the duck. Place the duck to the other side and cook slowly at a low heat until the meat is easily shreddable. The duck should be well cooked. If you cook it at a low temperature, the fat will keep it moist.

When the duck is cooked, let it cool to room temperature, and then shred by hand into 1-to-2-inch strips. As you shred the duck, be careful to discard any fat, tendons, skin, and gristle.

To make the Flautas: In a mixing bowl, toss together shredded duck, cilantro, green onions, 2 tablespoons of Mango Sauce, salt, and pepper. Lightly fry tortillas in hot oil (300 degrees F) for a few seconds until soft and pliable, and then drain on paper towels. As with enchiladas, place a small amount of filling (about 3 tablespoons) into each tortilla, roll, and secure end flaps with toothpicks. The flautas should be long and thin. Place ½ to 1 inch of oil in a pan. Fry flautas in oil until the tortillas are crunchy. Drain on paper towels at an angle so that any grease drips out the ends. Serve with Mango Sauce on the side. Makes 16 flautas.

 *"Flautas" mean "flutes" in Spanish.*

SMOKED DUCK FLAUTAS WITH MANGO SAUCE

INDIAN SHRIMP FRITTERS

Indian Shrimp Fritters

PREP TIME: 1 hour

TURNOUT TIME: 5 to 10 minutes

FEEDS: 4 as an entrée, 8 as an appetizer

The Tamatar Chutney may be prepared the day before or the morning of. Prepare Shrimp Marinade 2 hours in advance of cooking.

To make the Tamatar Chutney: Heat oil in a skillet. Cook mustard seeds in oil until they start popping. Add the asafedita, onion, and ginger; cook over medium heat until the onion is translucent. Stir in tomatoes and remaining ingredients. Raise heat and bring to a boil; turn down heat and simmer for about 20 minutes.

To make the Shrimp Marinade: Place ginger, garlic, and jalapeño in a bowl. Add lemon juice and salt. Toss with shrimp and refrigerate for about 2 hours before frying.

To make the Batter: Whisk together all ingredients in a medium bowl. Batter should be thin. You may need to add a little extra water to get the right consistency. The coating should be thin and tempura-like.

Heat ¾ to 1 inch oil in a cast-iron skillet. Test oil for proper temperature with a few drops of batter; the oil should bubble immediately and the batter should set quickly. If you are using a thermometer, it should read about 350 degrees F. Roll the shrimp in cornstarch; shake off excess. Holding each shrimp by the tail, dip it in batter, letting excess drip back into batter container. Drop shrimp into hot oil. If the pan is shallow, do this gently so the batter will not stick to the bottom. (If it does, do not touch it for about a minute. Let a crust form, then gently release shrimp with a spatula.) Fry in batches of about 6 shrimp. Fry for about 30 to 45 seconds on one side, then turn and cook for another 30 to 45 seconds before testing for doneness. Shrimp are done when they are opaque all the way through. Remove and drain on a paper bag or paper towels. Serve with Tamatar Chutney on the side for dipping.

> Use this recipe as a way to get to know your Indian grocer. The chickpea flour will be there as well as the asafetida. Asafetida is a pungent carrot-shaped tap root; it's commonly used in India, Afghanistan, and Iran.

 Chickpea flour is also known as chana besan.

TAMATAR CHUTNEY
2 tablespoons canola oil
1½ tablespoons black mustard seeds
⅛ teaspoon asafetida
1 cup finely diced yellow onions
¼ cup peeled and diced fresh ginger
2 pounds tomatoes, diced
1 teaspoon salt
⅛ teaspoon cayenne
2 tablespoons lemon juice
¼ cup sugar

SHRIMP MARINADE
1 tablespoon minced fresh ginger
1½ teaspoons minced garlic
1 jalapeño, seeded and minced
2 tablespoons lemon juice
½ teaspoon salt
1 pound shrimp, peeled and deveined, tails on

BATTER
1½ cups cornstarch, set aside ½ cup for dusting shrimp
¼ cup chickpea flour
3 tablespoons vegetable oil
¼ teaspoon red pepper flakes
½ teaspoon salt
1 tablespoon ground pepper
2 eggs
½ cup water
2 tablespoons vegetable oil for chutney + more for frying

3 ounces Mexican chorizo

4 cups Asadero cheese

2 to 3 scallions, diced

½ poblano chile, diced

½ red jalapeño, diced

1 cup black beans

½ cup roasted corn

½ cup diced tomato

1 tablespoon Cotija cheese*

Flour or corn tortillas for
    serving

*Pecorino may be substituted for
Cotija.*

QUESO FUNDIDO WITH VEGGIES

PREP TIME: 20 minutes

TURNOUT TIME: 10 minutes

FEEDS: 4 to 6

Take chorizo out of casing and crumble as you cook it in a pan with a little oil.

Place a 6-to-8-inch casserole in an oven preheated to 375 degrees F. Mix all ingredients except Cotija cheese, chorizo, and tortillas together in a large bowl. Place cooked chorizo on the bottom of the casserole. Add cheese mixture on top. Sprinkle with Cotija. Turn on broiler and let cheese melt to form a light crust on top. This dish should be served bubbling hot. Spoon the Fundido over the tortillas and fold them. Traditionally, it is served with flour tortillas, but it is also good with corn tortillas.

We have offered up two versions of Queso Fundido, which is a Mexican fondue. One includes a medley of diced vegetables and the other features wild mushrooms. Both are brought alive with the addition of Mexican chorizo.

½ cup dried forest
    mushroom mix

2 chipotles in adobo

3 ounces Mexican chorizo

1 portobello mushroom

4 cups grated Asadero or
    Monterey Jack cheese

½ poblano chile, diced

1 tablespoon Cotija cheese
    (optional)

Flour or corn tortillas for
    serving

QUESO FUNDIDO WITH MUSHROOMS

PREP TIME: 20 minutes

TURNOUT TIME: 15 minutes

FEEDS: 4 to 6

Soak dry mushrooms in enough hot water to cover until they are soft. Dice, saving mushroom liquid for soups and stews. Dice chipotles, reserving adobo for later. Take chorizo out of casing and crumble as you cook it in a pan with a little oil.

To prepare the portobello: Remove stem, and then, using a teaspoon, scrape gills from bottom side of mushroom and discard gills. Brush portobello with oil, season with a little salt and pepper, and grill about 2 minutes per side on a sheet pan at 350 degrees F, or roast about 6 to 8 minutes. Let cool, and then dice.

Heat a shallow casserole or cast-iron pan by placing it in the oven at 375 degrees F. Mix together Asadero cheese, poblanos, mushrooms, and chipotles in a large bowl. Place cooked chorizo on the bottom of casserole, and then add cheese mixture. Sprinkle with Cotija cheese, if using. Turn on broiler and let cheese melt to form a light crust on top. This dish should be served bubbling hot. Spoon a tiny bit of the adobo sauce from the can of chipotles on top before serving. Spoon the Fundido over the tortillas and fold them. Traditionally, this dish is served with flour tortillas, but good corn tortillas are great with it too.

POLENTA CAKES WITH SMOKED DUCK AND WILD RICE

PREP TIME: 3 to 4 hours for the duck; 45 minutes to 1 hour for the polenta and cranberry sauce

TURNOUT TIME: 10 minutes

FEEDS: 8

This dish is a great use for smoked duck, duck confit, or just slow-roasted duck legs. Whatever method you use, be sure the duck is well cooked at a low temperature and easy to shred.

To make the Cranberry-Bourbon Sauce: In a medium saucepan, bring orange juice and bourbon to a boil; simmer for 5 to 10 minutes. Add remaining ingredients and cook until cranberries are just starting to break down. Don't overcook.

For the Duck Polenta: Combine stock, wine, and water and bring to a boil. Whisk in polenta. Bring back to a boil and then turn down to a simmer. Stir frequently and cook for about 30 minutes. After 30 minutes, fold in duck, wild rice, and butter. Season with salt and pepper. Continue cooking for about 10 minutes more until it reaches a creamy porridge consistency. Pour onto a greased baking sheet, keeping the polenta about 1 inch thick. Let cool until polenta is set. This will take 1 or 2 hours.

When the polenta is cool, cut into squares. Heat a cast-iron skillet and add some butter. Cook polenta cakes until they get crispy on the bottom. Flip and cook the other side. Arrange on a plate, top with Cranberry-Bourbon Sauce, and serve.

CRANBERRY-BOURBON SAUCE
1 cup orange juice
1 cup bourbon
1 pound cranberries
Zest of 1 orange
¾ cup walnuts, toasted and coarsely chopped
1 cup sugar
⅔ cup water

DUCK POLENTA
2 cups chicken stock
1 cup white wine
1 cup water
1 cup polenta
1 cup shredded duck
1 cup cooked wild rice
2 tablespoons butter
Salt and pepper to taste
Butter for frying

COATING
½ cup flour
½ cup cornmeal
Salt and pepper to taste

SQUASH BLOSSOMS
8 squash blossoms
1 cup goat cheese*
1 to 2 tablespoons chopped
    chives or other fresh
    herbs (optional)
1 cup buttermilk
4 tablespoons vegetable oil
1 recipe Tomato Coulis
    (see page 148)

*If possible, use a local artisanal
goat cheese.

STUFFED SQUASH BLOSSOMS
PREP TIME: 30 minutes
TURNOUT TIME: 10 minutes
FEEDS: 8

*Nothing says summer like squash blossoms.
If you have a garden with squash, then you
should have an abundance of these. Use the
female blossoms: they are the ones without the
zucchini attached.*

For the Coating: In a medium bowl, mix
together ingredients and set aside.

To prepare the Squash Blossoms: Remove
the pistil and stamen from the squash
blossoms, and also the little green spikes
where the top of the stem stops and the
flower petals start. Cut a little slit in
the flower and fill with goat cheese. (If
you like, you can mix the goat cheese
with chopped chives or herbs first.) Dip
blossoms in buttermilk and roll in coating.
Refrigerate for 15 minutes.

Heat oil, about ½ inch deep, in a sauté pan.
Add stuffed squash blossoms two at a time
and cook until golden. Turn the blossoms
so they cook evenly on all sides. Drain on
paper towels.

Place Tomato Coulis on a serving dish and
arrange squash blossoms on top.

SPICE MIX
1 pound butter
10 teaspoons pepper,
    coarsely ground
2 tablespoons minced garlic
4 bay leaves
1 teaspoon dried basil
1 teaspoon dried oregano
1 teaspoon salt
1 teaspoon mild chile powder
Pinch fresh nutmeg
4 stems fresh rosemary
Juice of 2 lemons

SHRIMP
1 pound medium to large
    shrimp, shell on
2 or 3 lemons, cut into wedges
Tobasco

BAYOU-SPICED SHRIMP
PREP TIME: 20 minutes
TURNOUT TIME: 5 minutes
FEEDS: 4

*This dish might be the easiest and tastiest dish
that I have ever come across.*

To make the Spice Mix: Melt the butter in
a small saucepan and add the spices. Cook
over medium heat for 5 minutes. Add
lemon juice and set aside.

To make the dish: Remove the feet from
the shrimp, leaving the shells intact.
Heat the Spice Mix in a saucepan. Throw
in the shrimp and cook for about 2 minutes.
When the shrimp are done, they will be
opaque all the way through.

Serve in a large dish or on individual plates
with lemon wedges, Tabasco, and towels
for cleaning your hands.

SHRIMP AND GRITS

PREP TIME: 45 minutes

TURNOUT TIME: 10 minutes

FEEDS: 4

Ahead of time: Prepare the vegetables and shrimp.

To cook the grits: Bring 4 cups of water to a boil. Place grits in a saucepan and add boiling water, stirring with a whisk. When the grits start to boil, lower to a simmer and cook according to package directions. This will vary depending on whether or not you are using quick grits. When grits are cooked, whisk in butter and add salt and pepper.

> **This is a classic low country dish, from the Charleston, South Carolina, area. At the Roadhouse we serve it as is, or topped with eggs for breakfast.**

In a sauté pan, cook the bacon over medium heat. When it is cooked, remove it from pan. Drain bacon fat from the pan, reserving 1 tablespoon. Sauté peppers in the reserved bacon fat. Add a little more butter, if necessary. After about 2 minutes, add garlic, and then a minute later add mushrooms; cook until mushrooms are soft. Add shrimp and bacon and cook for about 2 minutes, or until shrimp are cooked through. Add lemon juice, Tabasco, salt, and pepper. Taste for balance.

Dish grits into four bowls and top each with one-fourth of the shrimp mix. Garnish with chopped scallions.

High-quality grits are available through specialty food stores. Polenta may be substituted for grits.

1 cup diced red peppers
(large 1-inch dice)

1 cup diced green peppers
(large 1-inch dice)

2 cups sliced mushrooms

2 slices bacon, cut in 1-inch
pieces

½ pound shrimp, peeled and
deveined, tails on

4 scallions, chopped in large
pieces

1 cup grits*

4 cups water

4 tablespoons butter

Salt and pepper

2 teaspoons minced garlic

2 tablespoons lemon juice

Tabasco to taste

Salt and pepper to taste

1 cup uncooked rice
2 cups diced onions
1 cup diced carrots
1 cup diced celery
½ cup butter, divided
3½ tablespoons good-
    quality curry powder
1½ teaspoons turmeric
¼ teaspoon cayenne
2½ quarts chicken stock
1 quart coconut milk
2 apples, peeled and diced
3 cups cooked and diced
    turkey or chicken
Salt and pepper to taste
¼ cup flour
¼ cup chopped cilantro

MULLIGATAWNY

PREP TIME: 1 hour

FEEDS: 6

Cook the rice in 2 cups of water. Set aside.

Sauté vegetables in half of the butter. When onions become translucent, add curry powder, turmeric, and cayenne. Cook for about 5 minutes; add stock and coconut milk. Bring to a boil, and then reduce to a simmer. Add apples. When apples are soft, add the cooked turkey or chicken. Adjust seasonings for salt and pepper.

Make a roux with ¼ cup butter and ¼ cup flour. Whisk into hot soup, being sure to whisk out lumps. Bring to a boil and simmer for 5 minutes.

Place rice in the bottoms of six 12-ounce bowls, top with soup, and garnish with chopped cilantro.

SOUP
¼ onion, diced
1 clove garlic, minced
1 poblano chile, diced
¼ cup canola oil
2 tomatoes, diced
2 quarts chicken stock
1 teaspoon salt
½ teaspoon pepper
½ teaspoon Mexican
    oregano
¼ teaspoon thyme
3 tablespoons lime juice
1 boneless, skinless chicken
    breast

GARNISHES
Chopped cilantro
Sliced serrano chiles
Sliced avocado
Tortilla strips
Lime wheels

SOPA DE LIMA

PREP TIME: 30 minutes

COOKING TIME: 30 minutes

FEEDS: 6

This is a traditional soup from the Yucatan.

Sauté onion, garlic, and chile in oil; add tomatoes. Add the stock and remaining ingredients, including the chicken breast. When chicken is cooked through (about 5 to 10 minutes), remove. When cool enough to handle, shred chicken. Bring soup to a boil; reduce heat and simmer for 20 to 30 minutes. Add shredded chicken.

Ladle the soup into bowls and top with garnishes.

CHILE CORN CHOWDER

PREP TIME: 30 minutes

FEEDS: 4

In a dry cast-iron pan, roast tomatoes until charred on the outside and soft inside.

In a soup pot, sauté onion and 2 diced chiles in butter over low heat. Add tomatoes, 3 cups of corn, salt, pepper, and milk. Bring to the scalding point (when bubbles form around the edge of the pot and the milk starts to foam). Do not boil. Remove from heat and let cool. Puree in a blender. Return to heat and add remaining corn. Bring to a simmer and taste for salt and pepper.

Roast the remaining 2 chiles. When cool enough to handle, peel and cut into thin strips. Ladle soup into bowls and garnish with chile strips and Asadero or Monterey Jack cheese.

3 tomatoes
1 onion, diced
4 poblano chiles, 2 diced and
	2 reserved
6 tablespoons butter
5 cups frozen corn, divided
2 teaspoons salt
½ teaspoon pepper
1 quart milk
Salt and pepper to taste
1 cup grated Asadero or
	Monterey Jack cheese

SALADS

GRILLED ARTICHOKES WITH MUSTARD-DILL VINAIGRETTE 87

FRIED GREEN TOMATO SALAD WITH SWEET CORN VINAIGRETTE 88

AVOCADO-CITRUS SALAD 91

WILTED SPINACH SALAD WITH WARM SHERRY VINAIGRETTE 92

GOAT CHEESE BRUSCHETTA 92

ICEBERG SALAD WITH BACON-BUTTERMILK DRESSING 93

CARAMELIZED FIGS WITH PROSCIUTTO AND HAZELNUTS 93

ROADHOUSE HIPPIE SALAD 94–95

POTATO SALAD 95

ROADHOUSE VEGGIE CHOP 97

DIXON APPLE SALAD WITH POPPY SEED DRESSING 98

GRILLED ARTICHOKES WITH MUSTARD-
DILL VINAIGRETTE

GRILLED ARTICHOKES WITH MUSTARD-DILL VINAIGRETTE

PREP TIME: 1 hour

TURNOUT TIME: 15 minutes

FEEDS: 4

To prepare the Artichokes: Bring a 2- or 3-gallon pot of salted water to boiling. Add lemon juice. Using a serrated knife, cut off the top of each artichoke and pull off the outer leaves, leaving the stem intact. Cut each artichoke in half lengthwise and immediately place into the boiling water. (If you are not going to cook them immediately, rub them with lemon juice to preserve their color.) Make sure the artichokes are covered with water. Cook for about 20 minutes. The artichokes are done when you can pierce the heart easily with a paring knife, and the leaves are soft and pull away easily but are not falling off.

Gently drain artichokes in a colander, upside down. Let them sit for 15 to 20 minutes while they continue to release water. When cool, cut each artichoke in half. (You will now have fourths.) Remove the choke and cut off the last ¼ inch of stem.

Prepare vinaigrette and use half of it as a marinade.

To make the Mustard-Dill Vinaigrette: Place the vinegar and mustard in a mixing bowl. Whisk in the olive oil, pouring in a slow, steady stream. Fold in the remaining ingredients. Let the artichokes rest in half of the marinade for at least an hour or overnight. Yields 3 cups.

Light a grill. When you have an even, steady heat, drain the artichokes from the marinade and grill for about 5 minutes per side, until they start to blacken and develop a light crust. Reserve leftover vinaigrette to dress salad.

To serve: Place mesclun on plates and arrange artichoke pieces over the top. Spoon remaining vinaigrette over the salads. Garnish with pieces of roasted red bell pepper, capers, olives, and dill. Add pepper and salt.

ARTICHOKES

½ cup lemon juice

2 artichokes

MUSTARD-DILL VINAIGRETTE

1 cup red wine vinegar

4 teaspoons grainy mustard

2 cups extra-virgin olive oil

1 tablespoon chopped dill

1 tablespoon chopped capers

1 teaspoon minced garlic

Salt and pepper to taste

SALAD

8 cups loosely packed mesclun

2 large or 3 small red bell peppers, roasted

2 tablespoons capers

20 olives

1 tablespoon chopped fresh dill

½ teaspoon cracked pepper

Salt

Grilled Artichokes are a very versatile dish. They can be served as an hors d'ouvre or as the centerpiece of a salad. At the Roadhouse, we create a salad by serving them over mesclun with roasted peppers and olives.

**SWEET CORN
VINAIGRETTE**

3 ears corn

¼ cup sweet pickle relish

½ teaspoon yellow mustard

⅔ cup red wine vinegar

1¼ cups extra-virgin
   olive oil

¼ cup celery seed

½ teaspoon salt

¼ teaspoon pepper

**FRIED GREEN
TOMATOES**

2 large or 4 small green
   tomatoes

Flour seasoned with salt and
   pepper

1½ cups buttermilk

Cornmeal seasoned with salt
   and pepper

Bacon grease (optional)

Vegetable oil

SALAD

6 scallions, diced

2 stalks celery, diced

8 cups loosely packed
   mesclun or arugula

2 strips bacon, cooked

1 cup cherry tomatoes,
   halved

Fried Green Tomato Salad with Sweet Corn Vinaigrette

PREP TIME: 20 minutes

TURNOUT TIME: 10 minutes

FEEDS: 4

To make the Sweet Corn Vinaigrette:
Roast corn according to directions on page 16. When cool enough to handle, scrape kernels off one ear into a bowl. Into a separate bowl, scrape kernels off remaining two ears of corn and set aside.

In a food processor, combine the 1 ear of corn kernels, relish, mustard, and vinegar. Process and add oil in a slow, steady stream. Add celery seed, salt, and pepper. Yields 2 ½ cups.

To make the Fried Green Tomatoes:
Slice tomatoes into ¼- to ½-inch rounds. Toss slices in flour seasoned with salt and pepper, pass through buttermilk, and then coat with cornmeal seasoned with salt and pepper. Fry until crispy on the outside and soft in the center. Drain on paper towels. The traditional medium for frying these would be bacon grease. You may substitute vegetable oil. For my taste, I would use vegetable oil with the addition of a little bacon fat.

To make the Salad: Make a mix of the corn from the other 2 ears of corn, scallions, and celery. Toss mesclun in the vinaigrette. Top with fried green tomatoes, vegetable mix, bacon, and 4 cherry tomato halves. Top with a little more vinaigrette.

FRIED GREEN TOMATO SALAD WITH A
SWEET CORN VINAIGRETTE

AVOCADO-CITRUS SALAD

Avocado-Citrus Salad

PREP TIME: 20 minutes

FEEDS: 4

Toast pine nuts on a sheet pan in a pre-heated oven at 350 degrees F for 5 minutes. If you are using tangerines, just peel and pull apart the sections. If you are using kumquats, julienne. For pomegranates, peel and then remove seeds. Oranges and grapefruits are more work. Peel them; then with a sharp paring knife, cut out sections and discard seeds.

To make the Citrus Vinaigrette: Whisk oil into the vinegar and citrus juices, then add shallots, zest, salt, and pepper and whisk again.

Toss the romaine in the vinaigrette and top with avocado, chives or red onions, and oranges, tangerines, kumquats, or pomegranates.

This is a refreshing year-round salad. In the winter when other fruits and vegetables may be hard to find, all kinds of citrus are plentiful and at their peak. We like to use an assortment of oranges (be sure to include blood oranges if possible), grapefruits, tangerines, kumquats, and pomegranates in this salad. The mix depends on the time of year and our own personal whims.

SALAD

¼ cup pine nuts

2 blood oranges or
   3 tangerines, kumquats,
   or pomegranates

8 cups loosely packed
   chopped romaine

2 avocados, sliced

2 tablespoons chives

½ red onion, cut in ½-inch-
   thin slices

CITRUS VINAIGRETTE

¾ cup extra-virgin olive oil

2 tablespoons white wine
   vinegar

2 tablespoons lemon juice

2 tablespoons orange juice

1½ teaspoons finely diced
   shallots

½ teaspoon lemon zest

½ teaspoon orange zest

Salt and pepper to taste

...LAD

8 sun-dried tomatoes

2 portobello mushrooms

Brent's Famous Candied
 Pecans (see recipe on
 page 150)

8 cups loosely packed
 spinach

**WARM SHERRY
VINAIGRETTE**

2 teaspoons minced shallots

⅔ teaspoon minced garlic

¼ cup sherry

¼ cup white wine vinegar

2 tablespoons lemon juice

2 tablespoons Dijon
 mustard

Salt and pepper to taste

1 cup extra-virgin olive oil

Wilted Spinach Salad with Warm Sherry Vinaigrette

PREP TIME: 30 minutes

TURNOUT TIME: 5 to 10 minutes

FEEDS: 4

Cut the sun-dried tomatoes into strips. If they are hard, reconstitute in a little warm water. Remove the stems and gills of portobellos with a teaspoon. Brush each portobello mushrooms with olive oil and grill on a hot grill. If a grill is not available, slice mushrooms and sauté in extra-virgin olive oil. Prepare candied pecans.

To make the Warm Sherry Vinaigrette: Place shallots, garlic, and sherry into a small saucepan and bring to a boil. Turn down heat and simmer for about 3 minutes. Whisk in all of the remaining ingredients except olive oil and boil again; then turn off heat and slowly whisk in olive oil.

To serve: Place spinach, sun-dried tomatoes, and portobellos into a mixing bowl. Turn up heat on the dressing; when it starts to come to a boil, whisk again and ladle just enough dressing into the salad bowl to coat spinach leaves. Toss. Place in serving dishes, top with candied pecans, and serve with Goat Cheese Bruschetta on the side.

GOAT CHEESE BRUSCHETTA
Goat Cheese Bruschetta is a perfect complement to this salad. The bruschetta will only be as good as the bread that goes into it. So use a good-quality artisanal bread. Baguettes will do, as will any rustic, country or farmer's bread. Cut your bread into ½-inch-thick slices and brush with extra-virgin olive oil on both sides. Grill or broil in oven until the bread is starting to turn golden brown. Turn and repeat the process on the other side. Spread on your favorite fresh goat cheese. Serve with salad.

Iceberg Salad with Bacon-Buttermilk Dressing

PREP TIME: 20 minutes

FEEDS: 4

Iceberg has been a much-maligned lettuce over the past few years, but this salad will remind you why you loved it as a kid.

To make the Buttermilk Dressing: Whisk together all ingredients except bacon, and then fold in the bacon. Yields 2½ cups.

To make the Salad: Arrange one iceberg wedge on each of 4 serving plates. Top with dressing, and then garnish each plate with 2 bell pepper slices, 2 tomato wedges, 1 red onion slice, and 1 radish.

BACON-BUTTERMILK DRESSING

2 tablespoons diced scallions
1 teaspoon minced garlic
6 slices cooked bacon, diced
1 cup mayonnaise
1 cup buttermilk
½ teaspoon pepper
¼ teaspoon salt
¼ teaspoon paprika
1 dash Tabasco

SALAD

4 iceberg wedges
8 bell pepper slices
8 tomato wedges
4 red onion slices
4 radishes

Caramelized Figs with Prosciutto and Hazelnuts

PREP TIME: 20 minutes

TURNOUT TIME: 10 minutes

FEEDS: 4

Toast hazelnuts on a sheet pan in a preheated oven at 350 degrees F for about 5 minutes, or until nuts start to brown. When cool, crush hazelnuts with the side of a chef's knife or cleaver, or pulse quickly in a food processor.

Cut figs in half lengthwise. Melt butter in a sauté pan; add figs, cut side down, and cook over medium to medium-high heat until the bottom surfaces of the figs are caramelized. Remove pan from heat and let figs cool in the pan.

To make the Sherry Vinaigrette: Toast and then grind the fennel seeds in a spice grinder. Whisk fennel seeds together with remaining ingredients. Yields 1½ cups.

This salad may be served on a large plate or on separate plates. Place a thin, even layer of arugula on the plate, and then top with remaining salad ingredients. Lightly drizzle with Sherry Vinaigrette.

 This is a great way to show off fresh figs.

SALAD

½ cup hazelnuts, toasted and roughly chopped
8 figs
¼ cup butter
6 cups arugula
4 slices prosciutto

SHERRY VINAIGRETTE

½ tablespoon fennel seed
1 cup extra-virgin olive oil
¼ cup sherry vinegar
¼ cup red wine vinegar
1 tablespoon shallots, minced
2 tablespoons parsley

SALAD

1 ear corn

2 medium beets

2 cups summer green beans

1 avocado

2 tomatoes

2 small heads or 1 large head Bibb lettuce

1 cup cooked garbanzo beans

1 cup radish sprouts

1 Vidalia (or sweet) onion made into Onion Rings

Magic Mushroom Powder

VIDALIA ONION RINGS

1 Vidalia onion

1 cup buttermilk

Vegetable oil

¾ cup flour

¾ cup cornmeal

Salt to taste

¼ teaspoon pepper

SESAME DRESSING

8 ounces tahini

2 tablespoons soy sauce

1 teaspoon sambal sauce

2 teaspoons minced garlic

1 cup water

1½ tablespoons sesame oil

¼ cup lemon juice

ROADHOUSE HIPPIE SALAD

PREP TIME: What's time?

TURNOUT TIME: Time is relative

FEEDS: Your head

I love to make this salad in mid-summer, when there is a lot of fresh produce from the farmers market. Feel free to play with this recipe and come up with your own combination of fresh vegetables. The onion rings are an extra step, but they really make the salad special. We can never decide whether this salad is better with Green Goddess Dressing or Sesame Dressing, so we have included recipes for both.

MAGIC MUSHROOM POWDER In Santa Fe, we are blessed with a large variety of all kinds of edible mushrooms which have a variety of tastes and other qualities. When making this salad at home, I would choose direction from one of my heroes (Emeril, Baba Ram Dass, Martha Stewart, or Mario, depending on my mood). At the Roadhouse, we, of course, comply with all of the USDA and DEA regulations, so we use dry porcini mushrooms, ground with a mortar and pestle or in a coffee grinder reserved for spices. A little of this sprinkled on top of the salad adds an earthy aroma and can take your dining experience to a new level of consciousness.

Roast the corn according to instructions on page 16 and remove kernels. Boil beets, and then peel and cut into wedges. Blanch green beans in boiling water and cut into 1-inch pieces. Cut tomatoes into wedges, and dice avocados last.

To make the Vidalia Onion Rings: Cut onion into very thin rings (⅛ inch or thinner). Soak onion in buttermilk for at least 2 hours or overnight. When you are ready to cook, drain onions in a colander. Heat about an inch of oil in a cast-iron skillet. Mix together flour, cornmeal, salt, and pepper in a mixing bowl. Toss drained onion rings in mixture until they are thoroughly coated. Shake off excess coating and fry the rings until they are crispy and golden. Drain on paper towels. These onion rings may be fried up to half an hour in advance.

If making Sesame Dressing: Blend all ingredients in a food processor. If it is too thick, add a little more water to get the proper consistency.

If making Green Goddess Dressing (ingredients listed on page 95): Combine all ingredients and puree in a blender.

To serve the Roadhouse Hippie Salad: Place lettuce on salad plate and top with corn, garbanzos, avocados, tomatoes, beets, and green beans. Drizzle with dressing; then top with sprouts and Vidalia Onion Rings. Sprinkle with Magic Mushroom Powder.

 **A NOTE ON SALT: If you are making the Vidalia Onion Rings as a topping for the salad, use 1 tablespoon salt. If you are serving them as a side, cut the salt down to 2 teaspoons.**

GREEN GODDESS DRESSING
3 tablespoons lemon juice
½ tablespoon chopped garlic
¼ cup chopped parsley
2 tablespoons tarragon
2 tablespoons basil
¼ cup chopped green onions
½ cup chopped spinach
1 tablespoon fresh mint
1 tablespoon lemon balm
½ tablespoon salt
1 teaspoon pepper

POTATO SALAD
PREP TIME: 45 minutes
FEEDS: 8 to 10

Bring a 2- or 3-gallon pot of salted water to a rolling boil. Cut potatoes in half, then slice each half into ¼-inch-thick slices and cook until just tender. Drain and cool.

While potatoes are cooking, dice onion, eggs, celery, and red bell pepper. Mince parsley. Fold all ingredients together and season to taste.

2 quarts sliced medium red potatoes
¼ red onion
4 stalks celery
½ red bell pepper
¼ bunch parsley
3 hard-boiled eggs
½ cup sweet pickle relish
3 tablespoons yellow mustard
2 tablespoons cider vinegar
1 to 1½ cups mayonnaise
1 to 2 teaspoons celery seed
½ teaspoon paprika
Salt and pepper to taste

ROADHOUSE HIPPIE SALAD

ROADHOUSE VEGGIE CHOP

PREP TIME: 30 minutes

FEEDS: 4

To make the Veggie Chop: Roast corn according to techniques on page 16. Rinse black beans. If you do not have freshly cooked black beans, a good quality canned variety is an acceptable substitute. Dice all of the vegetables into ½-inch pieces (a little larger than the black beans). Mix together in a bowl with corn and black beans. Season with salt and pepper and set aside.

To make the Creamy Avocado Dressing: Place cilantro (leaves only), scallions, lemon juice, and garlic into the bowl of a food processor. Process until you have a paste. Add the remaining ingredients and finish processing. Yields 4 cups. This dressing will keep in the refrigerator for one week.

To assemble the Salad: Mix enough dressing in the bowl with the vegetables to lightly coat all of the ingredients. On each of four salad plates or on one large plate, place 2 lettuce leaves. Top with a portion of dressed vegetable chop. Garnish with tomato and avocado slices. Top with sprouts.

VEGGIE CHOP

1 cup corn, fresh ear or frozen

3 cups cooked black beans

¼ red cabbage, diced

1½ cucumbers, peeled, seeded, and diced

¼ jicama, diced

1 poblano chile

1 red bell pepper, diced

¼ bunch green onions, sliced

1½ carrots, peeled and diced

Salt and pepper to taste

CREAMY AVOCADO DRESSING

¾ bunch cilantro

⅓ cup roughly chopped scallions

⅓ cup lemon juice

1 tablespoon minced garlic

1½ avocados

1½ cups mayonnaise

1½ cups sour cream

¾ teaspoon pepper

¾ teaspoon salt

SALAD

8 romaine leaves

8 tomato wedges (for garnish)

4 avocado slices (for garnish)

¼ container radish (daikon) sprouts

POPPY SEED DRESSING

⅓ cup sugar

1 teaspoon yellow mustard
    powder

1 teaspoon salt

⅓ cup white wine vinegar

1½ tablespoons grated
    yellow onion and juice
    from onion

1 cup salad oil

1½ tablespoons poppy
    seeds

SALAD

1 head romaine lettuce

2 apples

½ cup Brent's Famous
    Candied Pecans (see
    page 150)

¼ cup raisins

DIXON APPLE SALAD WITH POPPY SEED DRESSING

To make the Poppy Seed Dressing: In a stand mixer, combine sugar, mustard powder, salt, vinegar, onion, and onion juice; mix on low until combined. Continue mixing while you slowly drizzle in oil. Stir in poppy seeds last.

To make the Salad: Layer lettuce, apples, pecans, and raisins on individual plates. Pour dressing over top.

DIXON APPLE SALAD WITH
POPPY SEED DRESSING

MEAT

ROPA VIEJA 102

HERB-CRUSTED STUFFED PORK CHOPS 103

GRILLED PORK CHOP WITH PLUM SALSA 105

CABBAGE ROLLS WITH MEAT 106

CARBONNADE FLAMMADE 107

SMOTHERED COUNTRY-STYLE PORK RIBS 108

ETHEL'S JEWISH POT ROAST OF BRISKET

WITH GRAVY 109

ROADHOUSE-STYLE PULLED PORK 110

LAMB FAJITAS 110

MEXICAN MARKET-STYLE STEAK 111

MEATBALLS 112

FISH

ASIAN GRILLED SALMON WITH FRIED RICE 113

MUSTARD-BASIL MARINATED SALMON 114

TROUT WITH MUSHROOM, PINE NUT, AND

SAGE STUFFING 114

HALIBUT WITH POSOLE IN SOUTHWESTERN

ROASTED VEGETABLE BROTH 115

GROUPER IN CRAZY WATER 117

JAMBALAYA 118

GUMBO YA YA 119

FRIED CALAMARI WITH PUTTANESCA

SAUCE 120

CHESAPEAKE BAY-STYLE CRAB CAKES 121

BASIC MAYONNAISE 123

TARTAR SAUCE 123

SAFFRON-LEMON MAYONNAISE 123

GARLIC AIOLI WITH SMOKY SPANISH

PAPRIKA 123

CHICKEN

CHICKEN 'N' DUMPLINGS 124

ARROZ CON POLLO 125

ROADHOUSE TURKEY MEAT LOAF 126

CHICKEN ENCHILADAS SUIZA 127

CHICKEN POT PIE 128

JAMAICAN JERKED CHICKEN 130

POULET Á LA DIABLE 130

ROADHOUSE BBQ CHICKEN 131

FRIED CHICKEN 133

POLLO PIBIL 134

CHICKEN PICCATA 136

VEGETARIAN

VEGETABLE ENCHILADAS 137

TOMATO CORN BISCUIT PIE 139

FRITO PIE WITH CALABACITAS 140

VEGETARIAN CABBAGE ROLLS 141

MOROCCAN BUTTERNUT SQUASH STEW

WITH CHICKPEAS AND SPINACH 142

MEAT

MEAT

1 3-pound skirt steak, cut in
    6-inch lengths

3 14-ounce cans beef
    consommé (no MSG)

2 cups red wine

1 onion, cut in large dice

2 carrots, cut in large dice

¼ cup whole garlic cloves

2 bay leaves

1 tablespoon peppercorns

1 teaspoon cumin seed

Water to cover

SAUCE

1½ onions, cut in half
    lengthwise, then sliced
    into ¼-inch strips

2 green bell peppers, sliced
    into ¼-inch strips

2 red bell peppers, sliced
    into ¼-inch strips

¼ cup minced garlic

½ cup extra-virgin olive oil

2 tablespoons good quality
    Spanish paprika

⅛ teaspoon cayenne

1 tablespoon cumin

1 teaspoon salt

1 teaspoon pepper

1 28-ounce can tomatoes,
    pulsed in a food processor

2 cups white wine

ROPA VIEJA

PREP TIME: 2½ hours

TURNOUT TIME: 30 minutes

FEEDS: 8

This is a classic Cuban dish. Ropa Vieja means "old clothes." It describes the shreds of meat, peppers, and onions that resemble a mess of colorful rags. This dish is easy to prepare but takes a long time to cook, so plan ahead.

To make the Meat: Place all ingredients for meat in a stockpot or braising pan. Add enough water to cover. Bring to a boil, and then turn down to a simmer and cook until beef can be shredded with a fork. This will take about 2 hours. Let cool; then shred the meat. Reserve the broth. You may cook the meat ahead of time. Reduce reserved broth until you have half of the original volume.

To make the Sauce: Sauté onions, bell peppers, and garlic in olive oil. When vegetables start to soften, add the remaining ingredients for sauce; then add the reserved broth.

Bring to a boil and then turn down the heat to a simmer; let the sauce simmer. Add shredded beef and cook at a simmer for 20 to 30 minutes more. Adjust salt, cumin, and paprika to taste. (The cayenne should give the meat a little liveliness, but this is not a hot and spicy dish.) The end result should be moist but not soupy. If too much liquid remains, drain excess into a saucepan. Reduce over medium heat; then add reduced broth to enrich the dish.

At the Roadhouse we serve this dish with "Moors and Christians," which is simply white rice mixed with black beans. Another side dish we like to serve with this is grilled bananas. Our preference instead of regular bananas is always plantains when we can find them ripe enough. This can be a problem, so we sometimes substitute grilled red bananas, which are readily available.

HERB-CRUSTED STUFFED PORK CHOPS

PREP TIME: 45 minutes

TURNOUT TIME: 30 minutes

FEEDS: 6

To make the Stuffing: Peel and dice the apples. Remove the top and core of fennel and discard. Dice the fennel bulb into ¼-inch cubes. Dice the onion in ¼-inch cubes. Sauté the bacon in butter; add the apples, fennel, ginger, and garlic; cook over low heat until soft. Add the bread crumbs, stock, vinegar, sugar, salt, and pepper. Turn off the heat. Stuffing can be prepared ahead of time.

To make the Herb Mix: Combine all ingredients in a small bowl.

To make the Pork Chops: Make a slit in the middle of each pork chop and rub with herb mix inside and out. Stuff each pork chop with ½ cup of stuffing. Bake chops in a casserole at 350 degrees F for 15 minutes. Turn and bake for another 8 to 10 minutes. Place a meat thermometer at the part of the chop where the bones meet at a right angle. The internal temperature should be 145 to 150 degrees F.

> If you are dicing the apples ahead of time, store them in water laced with either lemon juice or apple cider vinegar. This will keep them from turning brown.

STUFFING

2 apples

1 fennel bulb

1 onion

¼ cup diced bacon

2 tablespoons butter

1 tablespoon grated ginger

½ tablespoon minced garlic

½ cup Japanese bread crumbs (panko)

½ cup chicken stock

2 tablespoons apple cider vinegar

¼ cup sugar

½ teaspoon salt

⅛ teaspoon pepper

HERB MIX

1 tablespoon fresh thyme

1 tablespoon fresh rosemary

1 tablespoon fresh sage

1 tablespoon minced garlic

1 teaspoon salt

½ teaspoon pepper

PORK CHOPS

6 (1½-inch thick) loin chops

Grilled Pork Chop with Plum Salsa

PREP TIME: 20 minutes
TURNOUT TIME: 30 minutes
FEEDS: 4

This dish should only be made with great, ripe fruit that is in season. You can also make this same salsa using apricots or pluots with delicious results.

Pluots are a complex hybrid of plums and apricots. Pluots are smooth skinned, like plums.

To make the Pork Chops: Grill pork chops outside on a grill for about 5 minutes over medium-high heat. Turn and grill for another 3 minutes; serve topped with salsa.

To make the Plum Salsa: Cut plums in half and remove pits. Then cut them into ½-inch wedges and place them in a mixing bowl. Cut onion in half lengthwise, then julienne into long strips. Dice jalapeño and sage; add to bowl. Add lemon juice, salt, and pepper to bowl and toss to mix.

The salsa can be made up to an hour in advance, but not too far in advance because the lemon juice breaks down the fruit.

PORK CHOPS
4 pork chops, ¾ to 1 inch thick each

PLUM SALSA
3 plums
¼ small red onion
½ to 1 red jalapeño
1½ teaspoons sage
1 tablespoon lemon juice
¼ teaspoon salt
⅛ teaspoon pepper

FILLING

⅓ cup diced onion

2 teaspoons minced garlic

2 tablespoons vegetable oil

½ pound ground pork

½ pound ground veal

½ pound ground beef

⅔ cup cooked rice

2 tablespoons raisins

1 egg

2 teaspoons good quality
    Hungarian paprika

½ bunch parsley, chopped

Salt and pepper to taste

SAUCE

1 onion

4 tablespoons butter

1 tablespoon garlic

1 28-ounce can tomatoes,
    blended

2 tablespoons sugar

4 tablespoons white distilled
    vinegar

1 teaspoon salt

½ teaspoon pepper

1 teaspoon good quality
    Hungarian paprika

¼ teaspoon thyme

1 teaspoon cinnamon

CABBAGE

1 head cabbage

CABBAGE ROLLS WITH MEAT

PREP TIME: 1 to 1½ hours

TURNOUT TIME: 30 minutes

FEEDS: 6

This dish should be broken down into steps to make it more manageable. The filling and the sauce can be made ahead of time. You can put together the cabbage rolls the night before serving and bake them right before dinner.

To make the Filling: In a 5- to 6-quart pan, sauté the onion and garlic in oil until they lose their color. Add meat and break it up while browning until it is cooked in small pieces. A potato masher works well for this task. Drain off excess fat. Fold in the remaining ingredients for the filling.

To make the Sauce: Cut onion in half lengthwise, then slice it into ¼-inch strips. Sauté onion in butter in a skillet over high heat, and then turn down heat to medium-low. Cook until onions are sweet and caramelized. Add garlic. When the garlic is cooked, add the remaining ingredients for sauce. Simmer for about 30 minutes.

Bring a stockpot of salted water to a boil. Cut the core out of the cabbage and pull off the tough dark green outer leaves and discard. Dunk the whole cabbage in boiling water and cook until the outside leaves easily separate from the center. Pull the loose leaves out of the pot and repeat until you have removed all of the large leaves. When leaves have cooled, remove the hard center ridge from each leaf.

Fill each leaf with about 1 cup of filling, fold in the ends, and roll. Cover the bottom of a shallow casserole with some of the sauce. Place cabbage rolls on top. Top with remaining sauce, cover with foil, and bake for about 30 minutes at 350 degrees F.

CARBONNADE FLAMMADE

PREP TIME: 2½ hours

FEEDS: 8 to 10

This is a great Belgian dish: beef braised in beer. At the Roadhouse, we make this dish 2 ways—either with chuck pieces or with short ribs. They are both great. This dish can be made a day ahead. I always feel that with a good stew like this you will want leftovers, so I have expanded the recipe to serve 8 to 10.

Mix flour with salt and pepper. Dredge chuck in flour mixture. Shake off excess flour and then brown meat in oil in an ovenproof skillet over medium-high heat. Remove the beef and turn down the heat. Brown the onion, garlic, and bacon in the same skillet. Scrape the bottom of the pan to loosen any flavorful bits. Add beer and continue to scrape the bottom of the pan to deglaze.

Return the browned beef to the pan; then add the remaining ingredients. Bring to a boil, and then carefully place the whole pan into an oven preheated to 300 degrees F.

Cover and let the meat braise in the oven for about 2 hours until fork-tender. Remove from the oven and let the beef cool naturally in the cooking liquid. (You may continue to braise the beef on top of the stove, but be sure to turn the burner down low, so that you have a low simmer. Also be sure to stir and scrape the bottom of the braising pan regularly.) Skim any excess fat off the top.

Serve over cooked egg noodles or with a potato-turnip mash.

> If you want to make this recipe using short ribs, plan on 1 to 1½ pounds per person. Use the same cooking technique as described here. Your cooking time will be 45 minutes to 1 hour longer.

2 cups flour

Salt and pepper to taste

4 pounds chuck, diced into 1-inch cubes

1 cup canola oil

4 large onions, diced

6 tablespoons minced garlic

3 slices bacon, diced into ¼-inch pieces

5 cups beer (Belgian if you are feeling extravagant, and yes, you will notice the difference)

2 tablespoons fresh thyme

2 tablespoons salt

1 tablespoon pepper

3 tablespoons Dijon mustard

3 tablespoons red wine vinegar

2 cups beef broth

1 cup flour
Salt and pepper to taste
1 quart chicken stock
8 country-style pork ribs
½ cup canola oil
2 quarts diced onions
2 tablespoons minced garlic
1 cup diced celery
1 cup diced green bell
    pepper
½ cup flour
2 tablespoons salt
½ teaspoon pepper
1 teaspoon dry sage
1 teaspoon thyme
2 cups canned tomatoes,
    pureed
¼ cup apple cider vinegar

SMOTHERED COUNTRY-STYLE
PORK RIBS

PREP TIME: 2 hours

FEEDS: 8

What could be more Roadhouse?

Preheat stock in a saucepan. Dredge pork ribs in 1 cup flour seasoned with salt and pepper and brown in oil over medium-high heat. Remove the ribs and set aside.

In the same saucepan, sauté the onion, garlic, celery, and bell pepper until soft. Stir in ½ cup flour and the spices. Let the vegetables cook for another 2 minutes. Stir and scrape any flavorful bits of flour from the bottom of the pan.

Add the hot stock, tomatoes, and vinegar and whisk to incorporate flour. Bring to a boil, whisk out any lumps of flour, and then add the cooked pork ribs.

Bring the liquid back to a boil, and then transfer saucepan to an oven preheated to 300 degrees F and bake for 1 to 1½ hours. The time will depend on the thickness of the ribs. The meat should be fork-tender when finished cooking.

Serve with collard greens and Grits Spoon Bread (see page 155) or Whipped Sweet Potatoes (see page 154).

ETHEL'S JEWISH POT ROAST OF BRISKET WITH GRAVY

PREP TIME: 2½ to 3 hours

TURNOUT TIME: 30 minutes

FEEDS: 6 to 8

2 large onions

6 carrots

2 stalks celery

1 cup flour

Salt and pepper to taste

1 beef brisket, first cut

1 cup canola oil

2 cloves garlic, minced

½ of a 28-ounce can tomatoes

10 cups beef stock

2 bay leaves

1 ounce fresh thyme, tied together with kitchen string

My mother, Ethel, was very particular about her brisket; from purchasing (the first cut only) through to the cooking. When I first opened the Roadhouse, my parents came to visit. My 93 year old Uncle Lou from California flew in to meet them here. As a grand welcome, I made Ethel's Pot Roast of Brisket. When the brisket was delivered to my mother she sent it back because the portion was too big. Peyton told her just to eat what she wanted and leave the rest. She persisted and, as always, won this battle of wills. By the time her plate was downsized, my Uncle Lou's brisket was cold. He then returned his for reheating. For someone like me, who has little patience to start with, this was a true test. We continue to serve a big portion of brisket to many appreciative guests at the Roadhouse, who may or may not have their own Jewish mother to cook them a brisket.

Since then, I have worked hard to perfect the brisket recipe included here. I am sure that my mom would approve. As with any braised meat, be sure to cook it slowly over a moderate heat, keep it covered, and let it rest in the braising liquid before slicing. Most importantly, be sure to slice across the grain.

Cut the onions in half and the carrots into sticks. Cut the celery into large dice. Set aside. Mix the flour with the salt and pepper. Dip brisket into flour mixture, and then brown it in canola oil in an ovenproof braising pan over medium-high heat. Remove meat from pan and add onions, carrots, celery, and garlic and cook until the onions start to brown on the outside. Return brisket to pan and cover with tomatoes and stock. Add bay leaves and thyme.

Bring the liquid to a boil, and then carefully transfer the pan to an oven preheated to 300 degrees F. Bake for 2½ to 3½ hours. The meat should register 185 degrees F on a meat thermometer. Remove pan from oven and let meat cool in the liquids for about 30 minutes.

Remove the beef from the pan first and then the vegetables. Remove the bay leaves and thyme bundle and discard. Let the broth sit for about 20 minutes. The fat will rise to the top. Skim it off with a ladle. (If you put the broth into a narrow tall container, this will be easier to do.) Put the liquid, celery, and about a third of the onions and carrots in a blender and blend.* Season with salt and pepper. This is your gravy.

Slice the beef into ¼-inch slices. It is important to slice the meat across the grain or it will be tough. Heat up the sliced pieces of brisket in the gravy or in stock and serve with onion wedges and carrot sticks.

*Let the liquid cool before blending or the top of the blender will come off and the gravy will go everywhere.

1 (6-pound) pork butt roast
3 cloves garlic
1½ cups tomato juice
3 cups canned tomatoes
1 bay leaf
½ cup distilled vinegar
¼ cup lemon juice
1 onion, diced
2 tablespoons brown sugar
6 tablespoons
    Worcestershire sauce
½ teaspoon salt
¼ teaspoon cayenne
½ teaspoon cinnamon

ROADHOUSE-STYLE PULLED PORK

PREP TIME: 10 to 12 hours

TURNOUT TIME: 30 minutes

FEEDS: 12 to 15

This is a longer-cooking dish best done in a smoker. It can also be cooked in the oven or by using a combination of the two.

Put all of the ingredients in a roasting pan. Smoke the pork overnight (or start early in the morning) at a low temperature (about 200 degrees). After about 10 hours, the meat will start to fall apart. (Note: The time can really vary so keep an eye on the meat.) Once the pork begins to fall apart—the internal temperature should reach 185 to 190 degrees F—remove it from the oven, scrape off any remaining fat, and shred the meat.

Remove cooking liquid from the roasting pan and skim fat off the top. Return the shredded meat to the liquid and reheat. Serve pulled pork on hamburger buns with coleslaw and chips or potato salad on the side. I love the coleslaw right on the sandwich!

LAMB
1 small leg of lamb (about
    5 pounds)
16 small flour tortillas

MARINADE
3 cloves garlic
3 tablespoons mild chile
    powder
3 tablespoons Mexican
    oregano
1 teaspoon cumin
½ tablespoon salt
6 tablespoons lime juice
¼ cup olive oil

GARNISHES
Roasted poblano chile strips
Grilled onions
Guacamole
Beans

LAMB FAJITAS

PREP TIME: 30 minutes (prepare the day before)

TURNOUT TIME: 45 minutes

FEEDS: 6 to 8

This is a dish that I have made for years, first at my restaurant in Philadelphia, El Metate, and now at the Roadhouse. Unlike trendy recipes that come and go, it has not lost any of its luster over the years.

To make the Lamb: Unless you are an aspiring butcher, have your butcher break down a small leg of lamb into lean 1½-inch cubes.

To make the Marinade: In a food processor, mix all of the ingredients Toss the lamb in the marinade and let sit in the refrigerator overnight.

Soak wooden skewers in water for 1 hour. This will keep them from burning on the grill.

Thread marinated lamb chunks onto skewers and grill lamb over charcoal to desired doneness. Serve with flour tortillas and your choice of garnishes.

I love this dish with either Salsa Cascabel (see page 146) or Tomatillo Salsa (see page 146). Even better, serve it with both!

Mexican Market–Style Steak (or Roadhouse Tampiquena)

PREP TIME: 1½ hours

TURNOUT TIME: 30 minutes

FEEDS: 4

For this dish, we prefer to use a less common cut of meat such as flat iron steak, hanger steak, or even a top round, cut thin. A good quality sirloin or a New York strip would also be great.

To make the Spice Rub: Mix together all ingredients. Rub on the steak 30 minutes before grilling.

To make the Enchiladas: Take about 1 cup of mole and put it into a shallow bowl about the size of a tortilla. Mix in about 2 tablespoons of water. Grate the queso Oaxaqueno or Asadero and process the Cotija in a food processor with a blade. It should look like grated Parmesan.

Heat the oil in a small sauté pan and briefly fry each tortilla, about 10 seconds per side. Using tongs, remove each tortilla when it is soft and pliable, shake off excess oil, and immediately dip each side into the mole. Shake off excess mole and set tortilla onto a sheet pan. Place about ½ cup of queso Oaxaqueno or Asadero into each tortilla and fold in half.

Cover the tortillas lightly with mole and bake at 350 degrees F for about 5 to 10 minutes until the cheese is soft. Sprinkle Cotija on top.

While the enchiladas are baking, grill the steaks and top with roasted poblano chile strips. Serve with enchiladas, guacamole, more mole on the side, and flour tortillas.

SPICE RUB
1 teaspoon salt
¼ teaspoon pepper
¼ teaspoon chipotle powder
¼ teaspoon Mexican oregano

ENCHILADAS
6 cups Mole Colorado (see page 149)
2 tablespoons water
3 cups queso Oaxaqueno or Asadero cheese
½ cup Cotija cheese
½ cup canola oil
4 high-quality corn tortillas
2 cups guacamole, for serving
Flour tortillas, for serving

STEAK
4 to 6 (8 ounce) pieces of steak
4 poblano chiles, roasted, peeled, and cut into 1-inch strips

MEATBALLS

MEATBALLS

⅔ cup diced onion

1 tablespoon minced garlic

¼ cup extra-virgin olive oil

5 pounds ground meat

1¼ cups Japanese bread
    crumbs (panko)

4 eggs

¼ cup pecorino cheese

½ cup chopped parsley

1½ tablespoons fresh thyme
    leaves

¼ teaspoon cayenne pepper

2 cups milk

1 teaspoon salt

¼ teaspoon pepper

MARINARA

1 28-ounce can imported
    Italian plum tomatoes

3 tablespoons olive oil

1½ tablespoons minced
    garlic

Salt and pepper to taste

2 tablespoons chopped fresh
    basil (optional)

MEATBALLS

PREP TIME: 30 minutes

TURNOUT TIME: 30 to 45 minutes

FEEDS: 10 (2 meatballs each)

For this recipe, you can use only ground beef if you prefer. We prefer to use equal parts ground pork, veal, and beef.

To make the Meatballs: Sauté onion and garlic in oil until soft. Let cool and then mix well with remaining ingredients. Refrigerate mixture for about an hour.

Form meatballs using a ½-cup measuring cup. Place meatballs on a baking sheet that has been oiled with olive oil. Bake at 350 degrees F for about 20 minutes or until cooked through.

Remove meatballs from oven and toss them in a little marinara while still hot. Serve over pasta or on a hoagie roll.

To make the Marinara: Drain tomatoes and reserve juice. Pulse tomatoes quickly in a food processor. Heat oil in a saucepan and sauté garlic. When garlic is lightly golden, add tomato puree.

Bring to a boil, and then turn down heat and simmer for 15 to 20 minutes over medium heat. If the sauce is too thick, add a little of the reserved tomato juice. Season with salt and pepper. If you like, you can add chopped fresh basil to finish the sauce.

> These meatballs are also great with Italian Wedding Soup, which is made with rich chicken broth, garlic, escarole, ½-inch meatballs, and rice.

FISH

ASIAN GRILLED SALMON WITH FRIED RICE

PREP TIME: 1 hour

TURNOUT TIME: 20 minutes

FEEDS: 8

This is a wonderful grilled dish.

To make the Marinade: Blend together all the ingredients. Reserve ¼ cup and toss the rest with the salmon fillets.

The marinade will tend to make the salmon stick. Make sure to clean and oil your grill with a brush before cooking the fish. Make the marinade in advance and marinate the salmon for 4 to 6 hours before grilling.

To grill the Salmon: Clean and oil the grill. Place salmon on the hot grill, flesh side down. Cook about 3 to 5 minutes (depending on the thickness of the fillet). Brush fish with reserved marinade while grilling. If the flesh is charring, move to a cooler part of the grill. Turn and cook for about 3 to 5 minutes more, or until fish reaches desired doneness.

To make the Fried Rice: Cook the white rice ahead of time and let cool. The day before is ideal. Put the vegetable oil and sesame oil in a wok or large sauté pan and stir-fry carrots, scallions, ginger, and garlic. Add egg in a thin layer and chop it up into little pieces with your spatula as it cooks. When the vegetables and egg are cooked, add the rice and season with soy sauce, tossing all of the ingredients together when the rice is almost done. Serve the grilled salmon over the fried rice and garnish with pickled cucumbers.

 Garnish this dish with pickled cucumbers. To make pickled cucumbers, peel and seed a cucumber, and then julienne. Toss with rice wine vinegar.

ASIAN SALMON MARINADE
½ cup soy sauce

¼ cup sesame oil

⅓ cup rice wine vinegar

1 tablespoon lime juice

1 serrano chile

2¾ tablespoons diced fresh ginger

⅓ bunch cilantro

1 tablespoon minced garlic

SALMON
8 (6-ounce) fillets salmon, skin off

FRIED RICE
8 cups white rice, cooked and cooled

1 tablespoon vegetable oil

1 tablespoon toasted sesame oil

1 carrot, sliced

¾ bunch scallions, sliced

3 tablespoons grated fresh ginger

3 tablespoons minced garlic

2 eggs, whisked

2 to 4 tablespoons soy sauce

MARINADE

¼ cup fresh basil
    leaves
8 to 10 cloves garlic
¼ cup Dijon mustard
¼ cup grainy mustard
1 cup extra-virgin olive oil
1 tablespoon lemon juice
1 teaspoon salt
½ teaspoon cracked black
    pepper

SALMON

4 (6- to 8-ounce) salmon
    fillets, skin off

Mustard-Basil Marinated Salmon

PREP TIME: 30 minutes

TURNOUT TIME: 20 minutes

FEEDS: 4

This is another simple salmon dish that is one of Peyton's favorites. Make sure that your grill is brushed clean and oiled before cooking the fish, as the marinade will tend to make the salmon stick.

To make the Marinade: Process all of the ingredients in a food processor. Reserve half of the marinade and rub the salmon with the remaining half. Let the salmon rest in the marinade for 4 to 6 hours before grilling.

To make the Salmon: Grill according to instructions for Asian Grilled Salmon with Fried Rice (see page 113). Before serving, brush with remaining Marinade.

MUSHROOM STUFFING

¼ cup pine nuts
1 cup diced onion
6 tablespoons butter
½ tablespoon minced
    garlic
6 cups sliced mushrooms
½ tablespoon smoky
    Spanish paprika
1 teaspoon dried thyme
1 teaspoon salt
1 teaspoon pepper
4 leaves fresh sage, chopped

TROUT

4 whole (8-ounce) Ruby or
    Rainbow Trout*
2 cups cornmeal
Salt and pepper

*If you like, you can cut the head off and trim the collar bones.

Trout with Mushroom, Pine Nut, and Sage Stuffing

PREP TIME: 30 minutes

TURNOUT TIME: 30 minutes

FEEDS: 4

To make the Mushroom Stuffing: Roast the pine nuts in a sauté pan over medium heat or on a sheet pan in the oven for a few minutes at 350 degrees F until they take on a golden color. Set aside.

Sauté onion in butter slowly until almost caramelized; then add garlic. Sauté for a few minutes more and then add mushrooms. Then add paprika, thyme, salt, and pepper. Cook well to concentrate flavors.

In a food processor, process pine nuts until they form a paste or powder. Add sage, and then mushroom mixture. Process until smooth.

To make the Trout: Fill each trout with about ⅓ cup Mushroom Stuffing. Roll trout in cornmeal seasoned with salt and pepper and brown in an ovenproof skillet over medium heat. Carefully remove skillet from stove and place in oven at 350 degrees F for about 8 to 10 minutes or until the trout is cooked through and the stuffing is hot. Serve with Wild Rice-Roasted Corn Pancakes (see page 152).

Halibut with Posole in Southwestern Roasted Vegetable Sauce

PREP TIME: 2 hours
TURNOUT TIME: 20 minutes
FEEDS: 4

This is a fish dish that says Southwest. Over the years it has become one of the most popular dishes at Harry's Roadhouse.

To make the Veggies: Roast red and yellow bell peppers according to directions on page 16. Reserve 1 red pepper; cut the rest into strips. Roast poblano chiles according to directions on page 16. Toss shallots in extra-virgin olive oil. Place in a shallow casserole dish and add about ¼ inch of water. Roast for about 40 minutes at 350 degrees F until shallots are cooked through. Let cool and peel.

Toss the elephant garlic in the bowl with extra-virgin olive oil and wrap each head individually with aluminum foil. Roast for about 40 minutes at 350 degrees F until each head is soft and cooked through.

To make the Roasted Veggie Broth: In a large stockpot, bring the stock and white wine to a boil, and then add 1 whole red pepper, 2 poblano chiles, 2 cloves garlic, and 2 shallots. Reserve remaining roasted vegetables as a garnish. Lower heat and simmer for about 20 minutes. Add honey and let cool. Blend in a blender and season with salt and pepper.

Cook posole in boiling water according to package directions. When the posole pops out of its skin, it is done. Add 2 cups of the posole to the broth.

To make the Fish: Poach the halibut in the broth until cooked through, about 5 to 10 minutes. The time will vary depending on the thickness of the fish. When the fish is cooked through, place each portion in a bowl, cover halfway with broth, and garnish with the remaining roasted pepper strips, poblano chiles, garlic cloves, and shallots. Top with a dollop of Cilantro Pesto (see page 152).

VEGGIES
3 red bell peppers
2 yellow bell peppers
6 poblano chiles
6 shallots
¼ cup extra-virgin olive oil
2 heads elephant garlic

ROASTED VEGGIE BROTH FOR FISH
1 quart fish stock
1 cup white wine
1 tablespoon honey
Salt and pepper to taste

FISH
½ pound frozen posole
4 (8-ounce) halibut fillets

GROUPER IN CRAZY WATER

GROUPER IN CRAZY WATER

PREP TIME: 30 minutes

TURNOUT TIME: 10 minutes

FEEDS: 8

This is a classic Neopolitan dish that has become one of our favorite summer dishes. Aqua Pazza, or "crazy water," refers to the seawater in which the fish was traditionally cooked. Seawater is a rare commodity in New Mexico, so we have used our "culinary license" and substituted fish stock. (I now see fish stock being sold at our local Whole Foods store. Or you can always make your own.)

 NOTE: If you cannot find fish stock, substitute a mix of half clam juice and half white wine.

To make the Crazy Water: Put all ingredients into a stockpot and bring to a boil; lower heat and simmer for 20 minutes. This recipe should be made ahead up to this point and the fish should be poached right before serving.

To make the Fish: Poach the grouper in the broth until done, about 5 to 10 minutes. Time will vary depending on the thickness of the fish. Make sure that you are cooking the fish at a moderate temperature, not boiling it.

To make the Bruschetta: Brush the bread with extra-virgin olive oil and grill or toast it in the oven.

Place poached fish in bowls, cover with Crazy Water, and serve Bruschetta on the side. Garnish with chopped parsley.

 Get the best bread you can find for this dish and make extra bruschetta!

HARRY'S ROADHOUSE

*I recommend the pan-seared fish, of course
A grouper which just leaves me at a loss
For words, the way it blends into its sauce
So plump and succulent*

*In every mouthful, every tender flake
There are no taste buds it cannot awake
No appetite so keen it cannot slake
No tongue so impudent*

*It will not be completely overcome
No jaded diner's face so sad or glum
But will regain its equilibrium
Eating this sacrament.*

—Rosé

CRAZY WATER

2 quarts fish stock

1½ tablespoons chopped
    garlic

4 cups diced fresh tomatoes

½ tablespoon salt

½ teaspoon Italian red
    pepper flakes

FISH

8 (6-ounce) pieces grouper
    or gulf snapper

½ cup chopped parsley
    (for garnish)

BRUSCHETTA

8 slices of excellent Italian
    peasant bread

¼ cup extra-virgin olive oil

SPICE MIX

1 bay leaf

1 teaspoon salt

¼ teaspoon cayenne pepper

2 teaspoons oregano

¼ teaspoon white pepper

½ teaspoon black pepper

¼ teaspoon thyme

½ cup vegetable oil

JAMBALAYA

½ cup (¼-inch-thick half
    moons) andouille sausage

1 pound boneless, skinless
    chicken breast

1 pound shrimp

½ cup vegetable oil

1 cup diced onion

1 teaspoon minced garlic

½ cup diced green bell
    pepper

½ cup diced celery

1½ cups long grain rice

2 tomatoes, diced

⅓ cup pureed canned
    tomatoes

2¾ cups chicken stock

1 bunch chopped scallions,
    for garnish

JAMBALAYA

PREP TIME: 45 minutes

TURNOUT TIME: 30 minutes

FEEDS: 6 to 8

Mix together ingredients for Spice Mix.

Cut the andouille into half rounds and dice the chicken into ½-inch pieces. Peel and devein the shrimp.

In a 4-quart pot, heat vegetable oil and then sauté onion, garlic, bell pepper, and celery for 3 to 5 minutes. Add the spice mix and the andouille and cook for another 3 to 5 minutes. Then add the rice, chicken, and tomatoes and toss. Add the stock.

Bring to a boil then turn down to a simmer. When three-fourths of the liquid is absorbed, stir in the shrimp and continue to simmer until all of the liquid is absorbed. Garnish with chopped scallions.

GUMBO YA YA

PREP TIME: 1½ hours (3 hours if you make the chicken stock)

FEEDS: 4 to 6 (as an entrée) or 8 to 12 (as an appetizer)

Cook the duck or chicken in advance. At the Roadhouse, we buy duck legs and slow cook them in our smoker. The meat could also be cooked on a grill or simply roasted in an oven. When the meat is cooked, remove skin and discard it. Separate the meat from the bones. The meat will be used for the gumbo and the bones can be used for the stock.

For the ultimate stock: start with chicken broth and add the bones from the duck or chicken and the shells from the shrimp. Simmer for 1½ hours, drain, and then skim off any fat. Use this broth for your gumbo. (If you do not want to follow this step, just use regular chicken stock.)

To make the Roux: in a thick-bottomed pot heat oil and whisk in flour. Bring to a medium-high heat and whisk constantly. As the flour starts to cook, continuously whisk and scrape the bottom of the pot, being careful to remove any bits of flour sticking to the bottom.

Keep the pot over an even medium-high to high heat to ensure an even cooking process. The roux will go through a series of color changes—from beige, to reddish, to coffee color, to almost black. (Cajuns call these colors blond, red, coffee, and chocolate.) While this is happening, the thickness of the roux will change, getting looser, thicker, and finally looser again. Be careful not to burn yourself. If you get the roux on you, it will stick to your skin and give you a serious burn.

When the roux has reached the dark brown stage, add the diced vegetables; this will help stop the cooking process. The heat of the roux will quickly cook the vegetables. When the vegetables start to soften, add the spices and the diced andouille, chicken or duck, and okra, and then whisk in the stock. Bring the gumbo to a boil, lower the heat, and simmer for about 30 minutes. Taste and adjust the seasoning for salt and cayenne pepper.

Five minutes before serving, add shrimp to hot broth. They will cook quickly. Spoon gumbo into bowls over cooked rice and top with chopped scallions.

 For a great meal, serve Gumbo Ya Ya with corn bread.

> **At the Roadhouse, we like to make our gumbo with a really dark roux. It gives a deep nutty flavor to the duck and andouille and accentuates their smokiness.**

GUMBO

2 to 3 duck or chicken legs

12 to 16 ounces andouille sausage, diced

2 pounds shrimp, cleaned

2½ cups diced onion

2 cups diced green bell pepper

1¾ cups diced celery

¼ cup minced garlic

3 bay leaves

3 teaspoons salt

½ teaspoon cayenne

½ teaspoon pepper

¾ teaspoon thyme

¾ teaspoon oregano

1 cup sliced okra (frozen is okay)

4 cups cooked rice

½ bunch scallions, sliced

STOCK

2½ quarts chicken stock

ROUX

1¼ cups vegetable oil

2 cups flour

PUTTANESCA SAUCE

1 28-ounce can imported
   plum tomatoes
1 tablespoon minced
   garlic
1 tablespoon diced
   anchovy
¼ cup extra-virgin
   olive oil
½ teaspoon chile flakes
1 tablespoon capers
2 tablespoons roughly
   chopped kalamata
   olives
¼ teaspoon black pepper
¼ teaspoon oregano
1 tablespoon chopped
   parsley, for garnish

CALAMARI

1 to 1½ pounds calamari
2 cups buttermilk
1 cup Wondra flour
1 cup cornmeal
4 teaspoons salt
1 teaspoon pepper
Canola or peanut oil for
   deep-frying

PASTA

1 pound imported linguine,
   cooked per package
   directions

FRIED CALAMARI WITH PUTTANESCA SAUCE

PREP TIME: 45 minutes

TURNOUT TIME: 15 to 20 minutes

FEEDS: 4

We have included only a few fried dishes in the book simply because frying at home is not too popular these days. This recipe is well worth it. Use more or less calamari depending on your appetite.

To make the Puttanesca Sauce: Drain tomatoes and reserve juice. In a food processor, process tomatoes with half of their juice. Do not overprocess, as you want the tomatoes to have some texture. Sauté garlic with anchovy in oil. When the garlic is cooked, it will lose its hard white color. Add the chile flakes, tomatoes, capers, olives, pepper, and oregano. Bring to a boil and then turn down the heat and simmer for about 20 minutes. While this is cooking, prepare the calamari and the pasta.

To make the Calamari: Buy cleaned calamari. Cut it into ¼- to ½-inch strips and soak it in buttermilk for 15 minutes. In a medium bowl, mix together Wondra flour, cornmeal, salt, and pepper and set aside. Drain calamari and toss in the flour mixture. Shake off excess coating using a large-screened colander over your sink.

In the meantime, heat about 1½ inches of oil in a cast-iron skillet. Cook the calamari in the hot oil in batches. Calamari cooks quickly and becomes overcooked within a minute, so watch carefully. When the crust is set the calamari should be ready. Test by tasting, as the cooking time will vary depending on your oil temperature, the capacity of the burners on your stove, and how much calamari you put in the pan at a time. Lay the cooked calamari out to drain on a sheet pan topped with a brown paper bag.

To make the Pasta: Cook linguine in a large pot of salted water while you are breading the calamari. Toss the cooked pasta in the Puttanesca Sauce before serving. For an authentic South Philly–style pasta, just pour the sauce on top of the pasta. Top with fried calamari.

CHESAPEAKE BAY–STYLE CRAB CAKES

PREP TIME: 1 hour
CHILLING TIME: 1½ to 2 hours
TURNOUT TIME: 20 minutes
FEEDS: 4 (2 cakes each)

The key to a good-quality crab cake is in high-quality, fresh crabmeat and a minimum of filling. In the mid-Atlantic states where we grew up, everyone looked to the little crab shacks in the Chesapeake as the places to go for the best crab cakes. We would drink National Bohemian late into the night, arguing over who had the best crab cakes, just as in New Mexico we argue about whether you find the best chile in El Rito or Chimayo. Being from the mid-Atlantic states, we prefer blue crab, but Dungeness is also acceptable.

Let the crabmeat drain in a colander to remove any excess liquid. Do not press out liquid. Place crab in a mixing bowl and, with a light touch, break up meat and then fold in remaining ingredients. Refrigerate for an hour or so in order to let the bread crumbs absorb the liquids.

In a separate mixing bowl, mix together ingredients for coating. (Note: a little Old Bay is great, but too much is overpowering.) Set aside.

Remove crab mixture from fridge and form into cakes. Use a ½-cup measure to form them and then knock them out into your hand. Dredge the cakes lightly in the bread crumb mixture, shake off excess, and place on a sheet pan. If you are having trouble keeping the cakes together, add a little more bread crumbs to the mix, but be careful as the idea is to use as few bread crumbs as possible. Refrigerate again for 30 to 60 minutes.

In the meantime, make your sauce for serving. Plain crab cakes without a sauce or with a little lemon or mayonnaise are delicious. If you are a traditionalist, you will want to serve them with an American-style Tartar Sauce (see page 123). If you want to blow people away, try a Saffron-Lemon Mayonnaise (see page 123) or a Garlic Aioli with Smoky Spanish Paprika (see page 123).

To finish the crab cakes, sauté them in a skillet in clarified butter or vegetable oil until they are crisp and golden brown on the outside and warm in the center. Remember the crab is already cooked so you don't have to worry about cooking the meat.

CRAB CAKES
1 pound crabmeat lump
1 pound crabmeat back fin
1 tablespoon mayonnaise
1 tablespoon Worcestershire sauce
¼ teaspoon baking powder
1½ tablespoons chopped fresh Italian parsley
¼ teaspoon Old Bay Seasoning
1 egg
¼ cup Japanese or fresh bread crumbs
¼ teaspoon salt

COATING
1 to 2 cups Japanese or fresh bread crumbs
Pinch Old Bay Seasoning

BASIC MAYONNAISE

5 egg yolks
2 tablespoons lemon juice
½ teaspoon dry mustard
½ cup extra-virgin olive oil
1½ cups canola oil
½ teaspoon salt
⅛ teaspoon pepper or to taste

In a clean dry bowl of a food processor, place the egg yolks, lemon juice, and mustard. Process for about 30 seconds. Leave the blade turning and slowly add the oil, a few drops at a time at first, then in a slow, steady stream. When finished, season with salt and pepper.

TARTAR SAUCE

1 recipe Basic Mayonnaise
1 tablespoon lemon juice
2 tablespoons finely diced red onion
2 tablespoons finely diced parsley
1 tablespoon finely diced pickle or cornichons
1 tablespoon capers
1 hard-boiled egg, coarsely chopped
Juice from capers to taste

Fold all ingredients into mayonnaise; add a little caper juice to taste.

SAFFRON-LEMON MAYONNAISE

5 egg yolks
1 teaspoon chopped garlic
Pinch saffron (about 3 to 4 threads)
Zest of 1 lemon
½ cup extra-virgin olive oil
1½ cups canola oil
 Lemon juice to taste

In a clean dry bowl of a food processor, place the egg yolks. Add garlic, saffron, and lemon zest. Process for about 30 seconds. Leave the blade turning and slowly add the oil, a few drops at a time at first, then in a slow steady stream. Add lemon juice to taste.

GARLIC AIOLI WITH SMOKY SPANISH PAPRIKA

2 teaspoons minced garlic
1 to 2 teaspoons sweet, Spanish smoky paprika
5 egg yolks
½ cup extra-virgin olive oil
1½ cups canola oil

In a clean dry bowl of a food processor, add garlic and paprika to egg yolks. Process for about 30 seconds. Leave the blade turning and slowly add the oil, a few drops at first, then in a slow steady stream.

Smoky paprika is a wonderful flavor booster and is available from the Spanish markets in sweet, bittersweet, and hot.

123

CHICKEN

CHICKEN STEW
2 chickens (3 pounds
    each), cut in pieces
Flour for dusting
Salt and pepper
Vegetable oil for frying
3 cups diced yellow onion
1½ cups diced parsnips
1½ cups diced carrots
1½ cups diced celery
3 quarts rich chicken stock
Salt and pepper to taste
1 cup pearl onions
2 bay leaves
3 or 4 sprigs thyme
1 cup peas
2 tablespoons fresh dill

DUMPLINGS
2 cups flour
1 teaspoon baking powder
2 teaspoons salt
3 tablespoons butter, melted
2 eggs
6 tablespoons milk
1 scallion, sliced
Pinch cracked black pepper

CHICKEN 'N' DUMPLINGS
PREP TIME: 1 hour
TURNOUT TIME: 30 minutes
FEEDS: 6

To make the Chicken Stew: Lightly dust
the chicken pieces in flour seasoned with
salt and pepper. Shake off any excess. Heat
a braising pan and coat it with about ⅛ inch
of vegetable oil. Brown chicken pieces,
remove them from the pan, and set aside.

In the same pan, sauté onions, then add
parsnips, carrots, and celery. Scrape the
bottom of the pan as the vegetables cook to
prevent any flour pieces from burning. Add
stock, salt and pepper, bay leaves, thyme,
and pearl onions. Return chicken pieces to
the pan and bring liquid to a boil; then turn
down to a simmer. Cook for an additional
20 minutes. Be sure that all of the chicken
is cooked through.

To make the Dumplings: Mix flour, baking
powder, and salt together in an electric
mixer. Add butter and eggs; add milk last.
Stir to incorporate but do not overmix.
Fold in scallions and pepper.

Let the dough sit in the refrigerator covered
for 30 minutes before cooking. Drop dough
by golf ball–sized spoonfuls into boiling
salted water or stock. Cover pot and cook
for about 15 minutes until dumplings are
cooked through.

To serve: Place chicken and dumplings in
a bowl. Top with vegetables and broth,
and then garnish with dill and peas. Turn
your leftovers into a great soup—add more
chicken stock if needed.

Arroz con Pollo

PREP TIME: 30 minutes

TURNOUT TIME: 30 to 40 minutes

FEEDS: 4

Dice onion, bell pepper, and celery in large pieces. Dice the bacon crosswise into small ¼-inch slices; dice tomatoes.

In a large sauté pan or paella pan, cook the bacon with extra-virgin olive oil, then remove. Add the chicken pieces to the pan with the bacon drippings and brown; then remove and place in a bowl with the bacon. Again in the same pan, sauté the diced vegetables until tender. Add all remaining ingredients, except parsley.

Return the browned chicken and bacon to the pan. Cook on the stovetop or in the oven until the rice is done and the chicken is cooked through. Top with chopped parsley.

2 yellow onions

1 green bell pepper

1 red bell pepper

2 stalks celery

2 slices bacon

1 28-ounce can tomatoes, drained

2 tablespoons extra-virgin olive oil

1 chicken (4 pounds), cut in pieces

2 tablespoons garlic

1½ cups red potatoes, sliced ¼ inch thick

2 cups uncooked rice

1 quart chicken stock

2 bay leaves

Pinch turmeric

Pinch saffron

Salt and pepper to taste

¾ cup green olives, coarsely chopped

4 tablespoons capers

½ bunch parsley, chopped

½ cup finely diced carrots

1½ tablespoons vegetable oil

1 yellow onion, chopped

1 teaspoon chopped garlic

2½ pounds high-quality ground turkey

1 cup milk

½ cup bread crumbs

1 to 2 eggs

½ cup pecorino cheese

⅓ cup chopped parsley

¼ teaspoon dried sage

1 teaspoon kosher salt

½ teaspoon fresh ground black pepper

½ cup ketchup

ROADHOUSE TURKEY MEAT LOAF

PREP TIME: 30 minutes

TURNOUT TIME: 1½ hours

FEEDS: 4 to 6

In a skillet, sauté onion and garlic in oil until translucent. Add carrots and continue cooking until they are soft. Then set aside and cool.

Mix together the remaining ingredients, except ketchup, in a large bowl. Add the cooked vegetables once they have cooled down. Mix well.

Press mixture into a well-oiled loaf pan. Coat the top of the loaf with ketchup. Cover with plastic wrap and then a layer of aluminum foil.

Place the loaf pan into a larger baking pan and fill larger pan with hot water halfway up the sides of the loaf pan. Bake at 350 degrees F for 45 minutes and then uncover pan. Bake another 30 to 35 minutes. Use a meat thermometer to test for doneness. The internal temperature should read 155 degrees F.

Let meat loaf rest 15 minutes before slicing and serving.

Try to get a high-quality ground dark meat from your local natural foods store or farmers market. Ground white meat will dry out and become flavorless.

Chicken Enchiladas Suiza

PREP TIME: 1 hour

TURNOUT TIME: 20 minutes

FEEDS: 4

To make the Filling: Poach chicken in a pot of chicken stock or salted water. Remove chicken from pot; let cool. When cool enough to handle, remove skin and discard. Separate the meat from the bones, being careful to remove and discard any remaining tendons and cartilage. Shred the chicken by hand.

Sauté mushrooms in butter until soft. About halfway through this process, add garlic. Remove stems from cilantro and discard; then chop cilantro leaves. Remove garlic and mushrooms from heat and toss with cilantro, scallions, and shredded chicken. Add ½ cup Suiza sauce. Season with salt and pepper.

To assemble the enchiladas: put about 1 cup of Suiza sauce into a shallow bowl about the size of a tortilla. Mix in a little water. Heat canola oil in a small sauté pan and briefly fry each tortilla, about 10 seconds per side. Remove tortilla from pan with tongs, shake off excess oil, and immediately dip each side into Suiza. Shake off excess sauce and set tortillas onto a sheet pan. The tortillas should be pliable and soft.

Place about ½ cup of the chicken mixture into each tortilla and roll up. Place enchiladas into a casserole dish and top with remaining 2 cups Suiza sauce.

Bake at 350 degrees F for about 20 minutes until enchiladas are hot inside. Top with crumbled feta cheese or queso fresco. Serve with Refritos Negros (see page 147).

FILLING

1 (3½-pound) chicken

2 cups sliced mushrooms

2 tablespoons butter

2 tablespoons minced garlic

¼ bunch cilantro

4 scallions, chopped

½ cup Suiza sauce (see page 146)

Salt and pepper to taste

ENCHILADAS

3 cups Suiza sauce (see page 146), divided

2 tablespoons water

Canola oil for frying

8 corn tortillas

½ cup crumbled feta cheese or queso fresco

PIE DOUGH

2½ cups pastry flour

½ teaspoon salt

2 teaspoons chopped fresh
   dill

¼ cup + 2 tablespoons
   shortening

¾ cup margarine

1 cup ice water (without
   the ice)

FILLING

1 quart rich chicken stock

2 chickens (3 to 3½ pounds
   each)

2 cups diced onions

1 cup diced carrots

½ cup diced turnips

½ cup diced parsnips

1 cup diced celery

2 cups diced potatoes

1 tablespoon fresh thyme

½ teaspoon marjoram

1 teaspoon salt

½ teaspoon pepper

½ cup frozen peas

ROUX

¼ cup butter

¼ cup flour

EGG WASH

1 egg

2 tablespoons water

CHICKEN POT PIE

PREP TIME: 2 hours

TURNOUT TIME: 30 minutes

FEEDS: 4

To make the Pie Dough: Put flour, salt, and dill into the bowl of a mixer. Cut the shortening and margarine into small pieces and add to the flour. With mixer on low, work in the fat until the flour is crumbly. Quickly add the ice water all at once and mix just until smooth.

Portion out the dough into 4 discs and chill for one hour. Roll out the discs so that they are a little wider than the rim of the bowls.

To make the Filling: Heat stock to boiling in a large stockpot and then turn down to a simmer. Poach chickens in stock. Remove and let cool. When cool enough to handle, remove skin from the chicken and discard. Remove meat from the bones, taking care to keep the pieces large. Take your time and be sure to remove all of the tendons and cartilage from the meat and discard. Dice the chicken into spoon-size pieces and set aside.

Carefully skim all the fat off the top of the stock. Taste the stock. If it is not intensely flavorful, add the chicken bones back in and continue cooking or add some high-quality, MSG-free bouillon cubes.

Bring the stock to a boil and then turn down. Add onions, carrots, turnips, parsnips, and celery; simmer for about 15 minutes. Then add diced potatoes. When the potatoes are just cooked through, strain the vegetables. Reserve the vegetables and stock separately.

To make the Roux: In a heavy-bottomed skillet, melt the butter and whisk in the flour. Cook over low heat for 5 to 10 minutes.

Bring stock back to a boil and then thicken with the roux. Return vegetables to stock and add thyme, marjoram, salt, pepper, and chicken pieces. Balance the seasoning. You should have a great chicken stew. The recipe may be made ahead up to this point.

Butter the four ovenproof, rimless bowls. Place the pot pie mixture into the bowls and add 1 tablespoon of frozen peas to each. Place bowls on a sheet pan. Cover each with pie dough, seal around edges, and paint with egg wash. Make a slit in each crust to allow steam to escape while baking. Bake for about 15 to 20 minutes at 350 degrees F until filling is bubbling and the crust is cooked through.

CHICKEN POT PIE

JAMAICAN JERKED CHICKEN

PREP TIME: **30 minutes**

TURNOUT TIME: **1 hour**

FEEDS: **4**

JERK MARINADE

3 cups large-dice yellow
  onions

1 or 2 chiles habanero or
  Scotch bonnet*

¼ cup ginger, peeled

4 tablespoons allspice,
  ground

1 tablespoon thyme

1½ tablespoons black pepper

½ cup white wine vinegar

½ cup soy sauce

CHICKEN

2 chickens (3 pounds each)

*Using 2 chiles will make the
marinade very hot.*

"Jerk" is Jamaican BBQ sauce. You will see the Asian-Indian influences in this recipe.

Blend all of the ingredients for the marinade together. Reserve one-fourth of the marinade. Cut up chicken into serving-size pieces (or buy them that way). Marinate chicken overnight in the refrigerator.

Remove chicken from marinade and cook it on a clean, hot grill. The chicken will have a tendency to stick to the grill, so make sure grill is clean to reduce sticking. Brush the chicken with the reserved marinade while grilling, and again when it is finished. Serve with grilled pineapple and Jamaican peas and rice on the side.

 Jamaican peas and rice are black-eyed peas mixed with rice.

POULET Á LA DIABLE

PREP TIME: **15 minutes**

TURNOUT TIME: **30 to 40 minutes**

FEEDS: **4**

MARINADE

2 tablespoons Coleman's
  dry mustard

3 tablespoons water

1½ cups Dijon mustard

2 tablespoons minced garlic

Salt and pepper to taste

CHICKEN

2 cups bread crumbs
  (preferably panko)

1 tablespoon salt

1 teaspoon pepper

2 tablespoons fresh thyme

2 chickens (3 to 3½ pounds
  each)

 In French, anything that features mustard is "of the devil," thus the title "Poulet á la Diable."

To make the Marinade: Dissolve the Coleman's in water, then whisk in the remaining ingredients.

To make the Chicken: Mix bread crumbs with salt, pepper, and fresh thyme.

Cut chickens in half. Dip the chicken in the marinade to cover all over, and then dredge in bread crumb mixture. This may be done in advance.

Cook chickens for about 30 minutes at 350 degrees F. Place a thermometer in the center of the thigh, near the bone, but not touching it. The reading should be about 165 degrees F. I am always surprised by how much marinade and bread crumbs I use for this recipe. The mustard will mellow as it cooks. Don't skimp.

Serve half a chicken with scalloped or mashed potatoes and broccoli or green beans.

Roadhouse BBQ Chicken

PREP TIME: 30 minutes

TURNOUT TIME: 1 hour

FEEDS: 4

To make the Texas BBQ Sauce: Sauté onion in oil. Put onion and all of the remaining ingredients in a saucepan. Bring to a boil and simmer for 10 to 15 minutes. Let cool and blend. This can be made a day ahead and should keep in your refrigerator for 2 weeks or more.

To make the Spice Rub: Combine all ingredients in a bowl.

To make the Chicken: Cut chicken in half and rub with Spice Rub 1 hour before cooking. The key to cooking the chicken is cooking it with slow and indirect heat. This means you should use a smoker or a kettle grill with the coals on one side and the chicken on the other so that you get a smoker effect. No flames should come in direct contact with the chicken. Cook the chicken through; the time will vary depending on your grill or smoker. An ideal cooking temperature is about 225 degrees F.

When the chicken is done, brush with BBQ sauce and serve with more sauce on the side. Serve with corn on the cob and potato salad for a great meal.

TEXAS BBQ SAUCE

2 onions, chopped

4 tablespoons canola oil

2 jalapeños, seeded

2 chipotles in adobo

4 tablespoons minced garlic

1 cup ketchup

1 cup Worcestershire sauce

1 cup coffee

½ cup molasses

¼ cup apple cider vinegar

¼ cup lemon juice

¼ cup mild chile powder

2 tablespoons yellow mustard

2 teaspoons cumin

2 teaspoons salt

¾ to 1 cup water

SPICE RUB

2 teaspoons salt

¼ teaspoon pepper

½ teaspoon mild chile powder

¼ teaspoon ground cumin

CHICKEN

2 chickens (3 to 3½ pounds each)

Fried Chicken

PREP TIME: 30 minutes (evening or morning before)

MARINATING TIME: 5 hours or more

TURNOUT TIME: 30 minutes

FEEDS: 4

2 chickens (3 pounds each), cut in pieces
1 cup buttermilk
4 cups flour
2 tablespoons thyme
2 tablespoons salt
2 tablespoons pepper
Vegetable, canola, corn, or peanut oil for frying

The night or morning before you want to serve it, cover the chicken pieces with buttermilk and refrigerate.

In a mixing bowl, mix together flour, thyme, salt, and pepper. Dip chicken pieces in flour, shake off excess, dip in buttermilk and again in flour. Try to keep each coating light.

Place coated chicken on a sheet pan lined with parchment paper.

Pour about 1 inch of oil into a 12-inch cast-iron skillet and heat until the temperature is about 300 to 325 degrees F. Place the chicken in the skillet; do not crowd the pan. Turn up the heat temporarily, because the temperature will drop when the chicken pieces are added. Cook for about 8 minutes, turning chicken pieces after about 4 minutes. The chicken will be almost done and should have a nice light golden brown crust.

Drain well and place chicken on a sheet pan, skin side up, in an oven preheated to 300 degrees F. Bake an additional 8 to 10 minutes. The chicken should have a nice crunchy crust and a golden color. If done right, it will be grease free. Check with a meat thermometer—internal temperature should be 165 degrees F. Our fried chicken is great with biscuits and country gravy.

Coating may be done ahead of time. Store the chicken pieces in the refrigerator until ready to cook. If the coating gets too warm, it will tend to stick to the parchment. A cook at the Roadhouse knows he has arrived when Harry lets him cook the fried chicken.

PIBIL MARINADE

¾ cup achiote paste

1 cup orange juice

¼ cup lime juice

2 tablespoons minced garlic

1 2-inch stick canela

2 teaspoons salt

2 teaspoons pepper

2 teaspoons thyme

1½ tablespoons Mexican oregano

2 teaspoons anise seeds, ground

CHICKEN

2 chickens (3 to 3½ pounds each)

4 garlic cloves

4 serrano chiles

4 tomato slices

4 scallions, sliced

½ bunch cilantro

4 banana leaves

SALSA

4 tomatoes

1 garlic clove

½ onion

½ habanero chile, chopped

1 teaspoon oregano, toasted

Salt and pepper to taste

Water

POLLO PIBIL

PREP TIME: 1 hour

MARINATING TIME: 5 hours or more

TURNOUT TIME: 1 hour

FEEDS: 4

This is a dish that requires a lot of work. The good thing is that just about all of it can be done ahead of time.

> Yucatan cooking is some of the most interesting and unusual in Mexico. Its use of sour and hot almost reminds you of the flavors of Southeast Asia. The "pib" is the Yucatan pit barbeque. (Like the jerk marinades of Jamaica or the tandoors of India, these marinades are used at Harry's to really expand our definition of BBQ.)

To make the Pibil Marinade: Place all of the ingredients in a blender and blend into a thick paste. Makes 2 cups marinade.

To make the Chicken: Cut up chicken into serving pieces and place in marinade for at least 3 hours or overnight. Place chicken, 1 garlic clove, 1 serrano chile, 1 slice tomato, and one-fourth of the scallions and cilantro onto a banana leaf. Fold leaf into a packet and seal in foil. Repeat for remaining 3 banana leaves. Make packets ahead and let them sit in the refrigerator for a few hours to marinate.

Smoke or grill over a low heat for 1 hour to 90 minutes until cooked through. (If using a smoker, go light on the wood chips. This dish is best when slow cooked, but not smoky. Cook over low heat at 250 to 275 degrees F for about 1 hour. Chicken should be 165 degrees F).

To make the Salsa: Roast tomatoes, garlic, and onion in a dry pan according to directions on page 16. Remove from pan and process in a blender. Add habanero, oregano, and salt and pepper to taste. Add a little water as needed to get the salsa the right consistency.

To serve, remove foil and place banana leaf packets on plates and just begin to unfold. The orange-red of the chicken looks beautiful on the banana leaf. Serve with the salsa, Pickled Red Onion (see page 151), Tropical Pico de Gallo (see page 151), and fresh corn tortillas.

 NOTE: The achiote paste, which comes from annatto seeds, can be found in a Mexican specialty store. Banana leaves can be found in Latin or Asian specialty stores.

POLLO PIBIL

CHICKEN

boneless, skinless chicken
    breasts (4 ounces each)
2 cups flour
1 tablespoon salt
1 teaspoon pepper
2 tablespoons extra-virgin
    olive oil
2 tablespoons capers
2 tablespoons parsley
2 tablespoons butter

PICCATA SAUCE
1 tablespoon minced garlic
2 tablespoons butter
1 tablespoon extra-virgin
    olive oil
1 tablespoon flour
2 cups reduced chicken stock
½ cup lemon juice
Salt and pepper to taste

CHICKEN PICCATA

This is an easy, quick dish that we also prepare with monkfish. The traditional preparation is with veal. The piccata sauce should be prepared ahead of time.

To make the Chicken: Trim any excess skin or fat from meat. Place chicken breasts between 2 pieces of plastic wrap and pound lightly with a meat mallet or with the underside of a sauté pan. The chicken breasts should be between ⅛ inch and ¼ inch thick.

To make the Piccata Sauce, sauté garlic in butter and oil until just cooked. Add flour to make a roux. Cook for 3 to 5 minutes. Heat stock and whisk into roux. Add remaining ingredients and cook for 5 to 10 minutes more.

Mix together flour, salt, and pepper and set aside. Dust chicken with seasoned flour, shaking off excess. Heat oil in a sauté pan. Add chicken to hot oil and brown on both sides. Lower heat and add sauce. Simmer for about 3 minutes until chicken is cooked through. Add capers, parsley, and butter. Serve with rice pilaf or on capellini.

Vegetarian

Vegetable Enchiladas

PREP TIME: 1 hour
TURNOUT TIME: 15 minutes
FEEDS: 4

This is an unusual enchilada sauce that comes to us via our neighbor Deborah Madison.

To make the Red Sauce: In a dry pan, toast the peeled garlic cloves, and then the pasilla chiles. After the chiles are toasted, stem and seed them and soak in hot water until they are soft. Discard the water and reserve the chiles.

Roast the tomatoes as described on page 16. Toast the walnuts on a sheet pan in an oven preheated to 350 degrees F for about 5 minutes. Toast the oregano in a dry sauté pan. When the walnuts have cooled, grind them, along with the garlic, in a food processor. Add all remaining ingredients except onions and oil to food processor and process. Sauté onions in a little vegetable oil. When soft, add it to the puree. In a saucepan, bring puree to a boil, then turn down the heat and simmer for about 20 minutes.

To prepare the portobellos, snap off the stem and cut off the bottom, dirty part of the stem. Reserve the rest. Use a teaspoon to remove the gills from the underside of the mushroom cap. Discard gills. Dice portobello stems. Brush the caps with oil and grill. After caps are cooked, cut them into ¼-inch strips.

Roast poblano chiles according to the directions on page 16. When they are cool enough to handle, peel and slice into ¼-inch wide rajas.

Sauté the onion slowly in vegetable oil until caramelized, adding diced mushroom stems halfway through.

To prepare the chard, remove the bottom 2 inches of the chard stems. Dice the rest of the stem and set aside. Chop the leaves in 1- to 2-inch strips. Rinse both the stems and leaves, being sure to keep them separate. Cook chard stems with garlic in a pan coated with vegetable oil. As the stems start to soften, add leaves and allow them to wilt and soften.

To make the Filling: Grate cheese and combine all of the ingredients in a large mixing bowl. Taste for salt and pepper and adjust seasoning at this point.

To assemble enchiladas: Lightly fry fresh corn tortillas in oil and dip in Red Sauce while still hot and pliable. Lay out 8 fried and dipped tortillas one at a time. In each, place ½ cup filling and roll up to make an enchilada. Place enchiladas in a casserole dish. Top with Red Sauce and bake in a preheated oven at 350 degrees F for 20 minutes or until the filling is steaming hot inside. Top with grated Cotija cheese and serve.

RED SAUCE

10 cloves garlic
3 pasilla negros (Mexican chiles)
3 pounds tomatoes
¼ cup walnuts
2 teaspoons Mexican oregano
¼ cup red wine vinegar
1 teaspoon cocoa powder
1 teaspoon ground canela
¼ teaspoon cloves
1 teaspoon chipotle in adobo*
¾ teaspoon salt
1 red onion, thinly sliced
2 tablespoons vegetable oil

FILLING

2 portobello mushrooms
2 roasted poblano chiles
1 onion, sliced
2 tablespoons minced garlic
1 tablespoon vegetable oil
1 bunch red chard
2 cups Asadero cheese
2 cups black beans

ENCHILADAS

8 corn tortillas
½ cup Cotija cheese (reserved)

You can use more if you like the heat.

TOMATO CORN BISCUIT PIE

TOMATO CORN BISCUIT PIE

PREP TIME: 45 minutes

TURNOUT TIME: 40 minutes

FEEDS: 6

In a small bowl, mix together lemon juice, mayonnaise, cornstarch, salt, and pepper. Set aside.

Divide biscuit dough in half. Roll out half and fit it into the bottom of a 9-inch pie pan. Lay half of the tomato slices in the bottom of pie shell. Top with half of the cheese, corn, and herbs. Then top with the remaining tomatoes, cheese, corn, and herbs. Spread mayonnaise mixture over the top.

Roll out the remaining biscuit dough and cover the top of the pie. Roll the top and bottom edges of the dough together. Cut off any excess and pinch the sides closed with a fork. Cut six slits in the top of the pie. Brush with melted butter and bake for 30 minutes at 350 degrees F. The crust should be golden brown. Let cool for ten minutes before cutting.

2 tablespoons lemon juice

⅓ cup mayonnaise

2 tablespoons cornstarch

2½ teaspoons salt

2 teaspoons pepper

1 batch biscuit dough (see page 59)

4 tomatoes, cut in thick slices

1½ cups grated good-quality sharp cheddar cheese*

1½ cups fresh corn

1 tablespoon chopped fresh basil

1 tablespoon chopped fresh tarragon

1 tablespoon chopped fresh chives

2 tablespoons butter, melted

Cabot cheese is preferred.

STEW

1 yellow onion, diced
1 tablespoon minced
    garlic
¼ cup vegetable oil
4 cups diced zucchini
4 cups diced yellow squash
1 teaspoon Mexican oregano
1 teaspoon cumin
1 quart cooked pinto beans
    (canned may be
    substituted)
3 cups vegetable stock
2 cups prepared Red Chile
    (see page 148)
4 cups corn, fresh or frozen
Salt and pepper to taste
4½ cups Fritos

GARNISHES

Grated jack cheese
Diced tomatoes
Diced red onion
Shredded lettuce (iceberg or
    romaine)
Sour cream
Pickled jalapeño slices

Frito Pie with Calabacitas

PREP TIME: 45 minutes

TURNOUT TIME: 15 minutes

FEEDS: 6

Frito pie is everywhere in the Southwest, but it is almost always made with meat. Here is our meatless version that has become very popular at the restaurant. In some circles, the only way to serve a Frito pie is to slit open the bag of Fritos and pour the stew over it. This is the down-and-dirty way, or you can just serve it in a bowl.

Sauté the onion and garlic in oil until it is soft and translucent. Add zucchini and yellow squash. When zucchini softens, add remaining ingredients except Fritos. Simmer for 5 to 10 minutes. Pour stew over Fritos and top with your choice of garnishes.

VEGETARIAN CABBAGE ROLLS

PREPARATION TIME: 1 to 1½ hours

TURNOUT TIME: 20 minutes

FEEDS: 4

This is a hearty dish for the fall and winter. It can be time-consuming to make, but everything can be prepared ahead.

To make the Filling: Dice the onion, carrot, and celery. Soak the dry mushrooms in a cup of water for about an hour, until they are soft, then dice. Reserve the soaking liquid for cooking the rice. In a skillet over medium heat, sauté the onion, carrot, celery, and garlic in butter. When they are soft, add the fresh mushrooms and cook; then add the reconstituted dried mushrooms and red bell pepper.

Cook the wild rice and barley separately in 1 cup of water each. Cook the white rice in the reserved mushroom liquid, adding enough water to make 2 cups. You want to be sure that each of the grains is perfectly cooked. Toss them together with the parsley, dill, scallions, and paprika.

To make the Sauce: Blend the tomatoes in a blender. Sauté onion in butter in a skillet over high heat, then turn down to medium-low and continue to cook until they are sweet; add garlic. Cook until soft, another 2 to 3 minutes; then add blended tomatoes and remaining ingredients. Bring to a boil, and then turn down heat. Simmer for about 30 minutes.

Bring a 4-quart pot of salted water to a boil. Cut the core out of the cabbage and pull off the tough dark green outer leaves and discard. Dunk the whole cabbage in boiling water and cook until the outside leaves easily separate from the core. Pull the loose leaves out of the pot and continue this process until you have removed all of the large leaves. When they are cool, cut the hard center ridge out of each leaf and discard.

To assemble Cabbage Rolls: Fill each leaf with about 1 cup of filling, fold in the sides, and then roll up. Place cabbage rolls in a shallow casserole dish. Top with sauce, cover with foil, and bake for about 30 minutes in a preheated oven at 350 degrees F.

FILLING
1 onion
1 carrot
1 stalk celery
¼ cup dry mushroom pieces
1 tablespoon minced garlic
4 tablespoons butter
4 cups sliced fresh
    mushrooms
¼ cup diced red bell pepper
⅓ cup uncooked wild rice
⅓ cup uncooked barley
1 cup uncooked white rice
2 tablespoons parsley
1 tablespoon dill
¼ cup sliced scallions
1 tablespoon good quality
    Hungarian paprika

SAUCE
1 28-ounce can tomatoes
1 onion, diced
2 tablespoons butter
1 tablespoon garlic
2 tablespoons sugar
4 tablespoons distilled
    vinegar
1 teaspoon salt
½ teaspoon pepper
1 teaspoon good quality
    Hungarian paprika
¼ teaspoon thyme
1 teaspoon cinnamon

CABBAGE
1 head green cabbage

STEW

1 cup diced onion

1 tablespoon minced garlic

6 tablespoons butter

2 teaspoons salt

1 teaspoon black pepper

1 teaspoon ground ginger

1 teaspoon turmeric

1 teaspoon cumin

1 teaspoon cinnamon

6 cups butternut squash,
  peeled, seeded, and diced
  into 1-inch pieces

2 cups carrots, diced into
  1-inch pieces

2 cups quartered red potatoes

8 cups vegetable stock or water

Pinch saffron

1 bay leaf

2 cups cooked chickpeas

½ cup raisins

1 small bag fresh spinach

COUSCOUS

4 cups boiling water

8 tablespoons butter

½ tablespoon salt

4 cups couscous (use quick-
  cooking)

Fresh cilantro (for garnish)

MOROCCAN BUTTERNUT SQUASH STEW WITH CHICKPEAS AND SPINACH

PREP TIME: 30 minutes

TURNOUT TIME: 40 minutes

FEEDS: 8 to 10

This dish is heavy on the prep, but easy to make. The Harissa and the Charmula are condiments that should be served on the side. They can be made a day ahead. All of the veggies and the spice mix can also be made ahead. The potatoes should be cut at the last minute or stored in water to keep them from turning color. Couscous may be made ahead an hour or two before serving.

To make the Stew: In a 6-quart pot, sauté onion and garlic in butter until soft. Add salt, pepper, ginger, turmeric, cumin, and cinnamon; sauté briefly. Then add squash, carrots, potatoes, stock or water, saffron, and bay leaf. Simmer over low heat. When all of the vegetables are soft, fold in chickpeas, raisins, and spinach.

To make the Couscous: Boil water with butter and salt. Mix in couscous, cover, remove from heat, let sit 10 minutes, and then fluff with a fork. Serve Couscous in a bowl and top with stew. Garnish with cilantro and serve Charmula and Harissa on the side.

CHARMULA

1 bunch cilantro leaves

1 seeded jalapeño

½ tablespoon minced garlic

2 tablespoons lime juice

6 tablespoons extra-virgin olive oil

1 teaspoon salt

Mix all ingredients together in a blender.

HARISSA

¼ cup New Mexico mild chile powder

2 tablespoons minced garlic

1 tablespoon red wine vinegar

½ tablespoon salt

¼ cup extra-virgin olive oil

½ cup water

1 teaspoon cumin

½ teaspoon caraway

½ teaspoon coriander

Mix chile powder, garlic, red wine vinegar, salt, oil, and water in a food processor. Toast cumin, caraway, and coriander in a hot, dry skillet. Grind in a spice grinder and add to other ingredients.

TOMATILLO SALSA 146

SUIZA 146

SALSA CASCABEL 146

BLACK BEANS 147

REFRITOS NEGROS 147

COWBOY BEANS 148

RED CHILE 148

TOMATO COULIS 148

MOLE COLORADO 149

GREEN CHILE 150

MANGO SAUCE 150

BRENT'S FAMOUS CANDIED PECANS 150

HABANERO SALSA 151

PICKLED RED ONION 151

TROPICAL PICO DE GALLO 151

CILANTRO PESTO 152

WILD RICE–ROASTED CORN PANCAKES 152

MASHED POTATOES 153

YUKON GOLD POTATOES WITH ROASTED GARLIC 153

POTATO-TURNIP PUREE 154

WHIPPED SWEET POTATOES 154

GRITS SPOON BREAD 155

COLLARD GREENS 155

TOMATILLO SALSA

PREP TIME: 20 minutes

4 cups tomatillos
2 serrano chiles
1 tablespoon minced garlic
½ bunch cilantro
1 tablespoon salt
1 teaspoon pepper
⅓ cup vegetable stock or
water
½ avocado, diced

Peel tomatillos and blanch in a pot of boiling water until they are translucent. Let cool before processing.

Remove stems and seeds from chiles. Place all ingredients except avocado in a blender and process until smooth. Fold finely diced avocado into salsa.

SUIZA

PREP TIME: 20 minutes

4 cups tomatillos
2 dried chipotles
1 tablespoon minced garlic
½ bunch cilantro
½ cup cream
1 tablespoon salt
1 teaspoon pepper
⅓ cup chicken stock,
vegetable stock, or water

 *This Suiza is a variation of the basic Tomatillo Salsa above.*

Peel tomatillos and blanch in a pot of boiling water until they are translucent. Let cool before processing. Cut stems from chipotles.

Place all ingredients in a blender and process until smooth.

SALSA CASCABEL

PREP TIME: 30 minutes

1 tomato, roasted
½ onion, roasted
2 cloves garlic, roasted
¼ teaspoon Mexican
oregano
10 cascabel chiles
½ teaspoon salt
½ to ¾ cup water

Roast tomato, onion, and garlic as described on page 16.

Toast oregano in a hot, dry skillet until you start to smell the aroma (about 30 seconds). Stem and seed chiles, and then toast for 1 or 2 minutes on a hot grill. Soak toasted chiles in water until soft and then drain. Place all ingredients in a blender and blend to desired consistency. Add water if salsa is too thick.

 Sauce may thicken over time and have to be thinned with more water after it is made. After you add the water, adjust the salt and pepper.

BLACK BEANS

PREP TIME: overnight
COOKING TIME: 2 hours
FEEDS: 12

4 cups dry black beans
1 carrot
2 stalks celery
3 cloves garlic
1 onion
Water
2 bay leaves
1 teaspoon cumin
1 teaspoon pepper
1 teaspoon chile powder
1 teaspoon salt

Soak beans in water overnight. Drain and add fresh water to the pot.

Chop carrot, celery, garlic, and onion into large pieces, and then process in a food processor with as much water as necessary until all vegetables are in small pieces. Add processed vegetables and remaining spices to beans. Bring beans to a boil, then turn down heat and simmer, covered, for 1½ to 2 hours. Time will depend on the freshness of the beans. Remove bay leaves before serving.

> **Quick-Soaking Method for any bean recipe:** Cover beans in water, bring to a boil, turn off heat and let soak for 30 minutes. Rinse and drain. Then cook according to recipe.

REFRITOS NEGROS

PREP TIME: 30 minutes
FEEDS: 4

1 onion, diced
2 tablespoons vegetable oil
1 tablespoon garlic
4 cups black beans, cooked
Salt and pepper to taste

> There are two schools on how to make refritos. Some go for the ease of processing the cooked beans in a food processor. Traditionalists prefer mashing the beans in the pan, as they mix with the onions and oil. I prefer mashing the beans in the pan as they cook.

In a sauté pan, cook onion in oil over medium-high heat until translucent. Add garlic and cook for another 2 minutes. Add beans and incorporate. Mash with a potato masher, letting the beans absorb the other flavors. Cook down for 15 to 20 minutes over medium heat. Scrape the beans off the bottom of the pot to keep from burning. Season with salt and pepper to taste. If the beans get too dry and thick, add a little water or stock.

The flavors in refritos, or refried beans, are concentrated, and the portions should be smaller than when serving whole beans.

Cowboy Beans

PREP TIME: overnight
COOKING TIME: 2 hours
FEEDS: 12

4 cups dry pinto beans

3 slices bacon, roughly diced

1 onion, roughly diced

2 poblano chiles, roughly diced

2 teaspoons minced garlic

1 (28-ounce) can tomatoes in juice, pulsed in food processor

1 bottle dark beer

1 teaspoon cumin

1 teaspoon salt

½ teaspoon pepper

Soak beans overnight and then drain and rinse. Put into a 5-gallon pot, cover with water, and add remaining ingredients. Bring to a boil, then turn down heat and simmer, covered, until beans are cooked through, 1½ to 2 hours.

See quick-soaking method recipe on page 147.

Red Chile

PREP TIME: 2 hours
MAKES: 3 quarts

16 cups mild New Mexico (red chile) pods, dry and loosely packed

6 pasilla negros (chiles)

4 ancho chiles

4 cups hot water

1 onion

6 cloves garlic

1 tablespoon cumin seed, toasted

1 tablespoon Mexican oregano, toasted

2 teaspoons salt

¼ teaspoon pepper

Water, or beef or chicken stock

Red Chile is used with Breakfast Burrito (see page 64) and Frito Pie (see page 140). It can also be used with enchiladas and posole and makes a tasty addition to stews.

Toast chiles in a hot cast-iron pan for about 30 seconds per side, until they start to give off a distinct chile aroma. Cover with hot water and let soak until soft. This can be done early in the morning the day you are making the recipe or the night before.

In a cast-iron pan, roast onion and garlic over medium-high heat. In a separate pan, toast cumin seeds and oregano. Grind cumin seeds in a spice grinder.

Remove stems and seeds from soaking chiles. Discard soaking and rinsing water. Combine chiles, garlic, onion, and spices. Cover with water or stock, bring to a boil, and simmer for 20 to 30 minutes; blend. Optional: Pour red chile through a sieve.

Tomato Coulis

MAKES: 2 cups

2 large tomatoes

2 tablespoons extra-virgin olive oil

1 tablespoon chopped garlic

1 teaspoon salt

¼ teaspoon pepper

Coarsely chop tomatoes, then pulse in a food processor. Do not overprocess; leave some texture in the mix. In a small saucepan, heat the oil, and then sauté garlic. Add tomatoes, salt, and pepper.

Bring liquid to a boil, and then turn down and simmer for about 10 minutes. Let puree cool before serving. Serve with Stuffed Squash Blossoms (see page 80).

Mole Colorado

PREP TIME: 1 to 2 hours

MAKES: 3 quarts

Making moles can be a daunting task because the long list of ingredients can be intimidating. This is a fairly straightforward recipe. The key is in breaking the recipe into steps and being organized.

Toast chiles in a hot cast-iron skillet, about 30 seconds per side. Your kitchen will fill with a wonderful aroma. Cover the chiles with hot water and set aside for an hour or so until they are soft.

Roast onion and garlic with skins on. Cut onion into wedges and toast with garlic in the same skillet you used for the chiles. Let the onion get black and slightly charred on the edges. Do the same with the garlic. Set aside. When cool enough to handle, peel onion and garlic skin and discard.

Toast almonds on a sheet pan in the oven for about 5 minutes at 350 degrees F. Let cool, then grind in a food processor until they have a flour-like consistency. They should be golden but not burnt. Toast the dry spices in a hot cast-iron skillet for about 30 seconds. Let cool and grind spices in a spice grinder or with a mortar and pestle.

When chiles are soft, remove stems and seeds. Wash out the seeds by dipping chiles in the soaking water. Wear rubber gloves for this task. Drain and set aside.

Place all ingredients except the chocolate in a stockpot. Bring to a boil, then reduce heat and simmer for about 30 minutes. Stir in the chocolate and make sure it melts and gets incorporated into the sauce. Do not let it stick to the bottom of the pot and burn. Let the mole cool, then transfer to a blender and blend. (Do not attempt to blend the mole while it is hot or the lid will fly off your blender and you will burn yourself and have quite a mess in your kitchen.)

Coat the bottom of a stockpot with about ⅛ inch oil. Heat oil to the smoking point and then pour in mole. Bring to a boil. Taste for seasoning and add more salt if necessary. Turn down heat and simmer for 20 minutes. I like to blend the mole a second time to get the texture that I like. You can skip the second blending if you think it unnecessary.

In addition to the cheese enchiladas for the market steak, this mole is great with chicken enchiladas and huevos rancheros.

You can store extra Mole Colorado in the refrigerator for 5 days or freeze it for later use.

10 ancho chiles

1 onion

10 cloves garlic*

6 tablespoons blanched almonds

¼ teaspoon cloves

1 (2-inch) stick canela

1 teaspoon oregano

¼ teaspoon cumin

1 tomato

⅓ cup raisins

8 to 16 cups vegetable or chicken stock

1 slice stale French bread

3 tablespoons oil

2 teaspoons sugar (optional)

1 tablespoon salt

¼ teaspoon pepper

2¾ ounces Mexican chocolate

Oil for coating pot

The garlic can remain together as a head—you do not need to separate the cloves.

149

Green Chile

PREP TIME: 45 minutes

MAKES: 3 to 4 quarts

1 onion
1 clove garlic
2 tablespoons vegetable oil
1 (56-ounce) package frozen
   mild green chiles, chopped
1 (13-ounce) package frozen
   hot green chiles, chopped
1 teaspoon Mexican oregano
6 cups water or stock,
   divided
1 to 1½ tablespoons salt
¼ teaspoon pepper
3 tablespoons cornstarch

Green Chile goes well with chicken or turkey enchiladas and makes a mean green chile stew with pork.

Dice onion and garlic and sauté in oil in a large skillet until soft. Add green chiles, oregano, 5 cups of water or stock, salt, and pepper; bring to a boil. Turn down heat and simmer for about 15 minutes.

Whisk together cornstarch and remaining 1 cup water or stock. Turn up heat on the chile and whisk in the cornstarch mixture. Bring back to a boil and continue whisking for about 1 minute. Be sure there are no lumps. Simmer for about 5 minutes more. Taste for salt and pepper. The chile is ready to serve. It will store in the refrigerator for 1 week.

Mango Sauce

PREP TIME: 20 minutes

MAKES: 2½ cups

2 cups mango pulp
½ cup orange juice
2 tablespoons lime juice
2 serrano chiles
1 tablespoon chopped
   cilantro
2 tablespoons diced red
   onion
½ teaspoon salt
Pinch pepper

This sauce is used with Smoked Duck Flautas, page 74, and could also be a nice accompaniment for chicken dishes, such as tacos.

Peel mango and place pulp in a blender with orange juice, lime juice, and chiles; blend. Fold in cilantro, onion, salt, and pepper. More chile may be added if you like your salsa hotter.

Brent's famous Candied Pecans

TURNOUT TIME: 15 minutes

2 cups pecans
1 teaspoon vegetable oil
¼ cup sugar
¼ teaspoon salt
½ teaspoon mild red chile
   powder

I find it impossible not to snack on these nuts.

In a 10-inch sauté pan, heat pecans and toss with oil. Add the sugar and melt

over medium heat until sugar starts to caramelize and coats the nuts. Season with salt and chile powder and toss onto a sheet pan lined with parchment paper to cool. Keep in a single layer.

HABANERO SALSA

PREP TIME: 20 minutes

MAKES: 3 to 4 cups

4 tomatoes
1 clove garlic
½ onion
½ habanero, stem and seeds removed
1 teaspoon oregano, toasted
Salt and pepper to taste
Water

Roast tomatoes, garlic, and onion in a hot dry pan according to directions on page 16. Put in a blender, add remaining ingredients, and blend. You can add a little more water if the sauce is thick. Always wear gloves when handling habaneros.

PICKLED RED ONION

PREP TIME: 20 minutes

MAKES: 2 cups

2 red onions
½ cup apple cider vinegar
½ cup rice vinegar
4 cloves garlic
1 stick canela
1 teaspoon whole allspice berries
1 teaspoon cloves
1 teaspoon whole coriander
1 teaspoon anise seed
1 teaspoon whole peppercorns
1 teaspoon salt

This should be made at least a day ahead of time. Pickled Red Onion is served with Pollo Pibil (page 134) and is a traditional condiment. It is a great accompaniment to tacos, too.

Slice onions into ¼-inch rounds. Blanch in boiling salted water for about 1 minute; drain thoroughly and cover with vinegar. Mix in spices. Pickled Red Onions will last in your refrigerator for two months or longer.

TROPICAL PICO DE GALLO

PREP TIME: 20 minutes

YIELDS: 1 quart

1 pound jicama
2 cucumbers
½ pineapple, skinned and cored
1 mango
2 oranges
Juice of 1 lime
¼ cup olive oil
Salt and pepper
Pinch mild chile powder

Tropical Pico de Gallo is served with Pollo Pibil (page 134) and is also a nice accompaniment for fish dishes.

Peel and julienne jicama. Half the cucumbers lengthwise and seed, and then cut into half rounds. Dice the pineapple and mangos. Peel the oranges and cut into sections. In a large bowl, toss all ingredients together with lime juice and olive oil. Just before serving, sprinkle with salt and pepper and a little mild chile powder on top.

CILANTRO PESTO

PREP TIME: 15 minutes

YIELDS: 1 cup

1 bunch cilantro

½ cup toasted pumpkin seeds (pepitas)

1 tablespoon garlic

1 roasted poblano chile

2 tablespoons Cotija cheese

½ teaspoon salt

Pinch pepper

3 ounces extra-virgin olive oil

This pesto is served with Halibut with Posole (see page 115) and could accompany grilled fish, egg dishes, and salads.

Rinse cilantro and remove leaves; discard stems. Toast pumpkin seeds in a cast-iron pan. Place toasted seeds in a food processor and grind until they are powdery. Add the remaining dry ingredients and pulse until you have a dry paste. Add the oil and process. Scrape sides to be sure you have incorporated all the ingredients.

* Cotija is an aged Mexican cheese. If you cannot find it, substitute Parmesan or pecorino.

WILD RICE–ROASTED CORN PANCAKES

PREP TIME: 1 hour

TURNOUT TIME: 10 minutes

FEEDS: 4 to 6

2 eggs

2 tablespoons butter, melted

2 cups milk

4 cups flour

1 teaspoon honey

⅓ teaspoon baking powder

1¼ cups roasted corn

1¼ cups cooked wild rice

¾ bunch scallions, chopped

⅓ cup chopped cilantro leaves

¾ teaspoon chipotle powder

½ tablespoon salt

¼ tablespoon cracked pepper

This is a savory pancake recipe that is a favorite side dish for Stuffed Trout (see page 114).

As in any pancake recipe, whisk together dry ingredients and then fold in wet ones.

Cook the pancakes with butter in a cast-iron skillet. The batter may seem a little thin, but the cakes should cook just fine.

MASHED POTATOES

PREP TIME: 45 minutes

SPECIAL EQUIPMENT: food mill or potato ricer

FEEDS: 4

2 pounds russet or Yukon
  Gold potatoes
4 tablespoons butter
½ cup milk or cream
1 teaspoon salt
Pepper to taste

Cut potatoes into 2-inch slices. Place in a pot of boiling salted water. Cook potatoes until soft but not mushy; overcooking them will make grainy Mashed Potatoes. When the potatoes are done, work quickly. Drain and shake off excess water. Run potatoes through a food mill or potato ricer. Add butter while potatoes are still hot. If you like, you may run the butter through the mill with the potatoes. Fold in milk or cream, salt, and pepper. You will find that potatoes absorb a lot of salt and milk.

> At Harry's Roadhouse, when we make Mashed Potatoes, we do not peel them. This is your choice. We also add chopped scallions for taste and texture.

YUKON GOLD POTATOES WITH ROASTED GARLIC

PREP TIME: 45 minutes

1 recipe Mashed Potatoes
  (above)
1 head garlic or to taste

Prepare the Mashed Potatoes according to directions.

Coat garlic heads with oil and wrap in foil. Roast in the oven at 350 degrees F until soft, about 30 to 40 minutes. Let cool; cut in half and squeeze out the roasted cloves.

Puree garlic cloves in a food processor. Fold 3 tablespoons puree into Mashed Potatoes while they are hot.

POTATO-TURNIP PUREE

PREP TIME: 45 minutes

SPECIAL EQUIPMENT: food mill or potato ricer

FEEDS: 4

1 pound turnips

2 pounds russet potatoes

¼ cup cream

3 tablespoons butter

1½ teaspoons salt

2 tablespoons heavy cream

¼ teaspoon pepper

 I like to use peeled potatoes for this recipe. I was first exposed to this dish as "Shakers Alabaster."

Peel turnips and potatoes. Cut into 2-inch slices. Place turnips and potatoes in separate pots of boiling salted water. Cook until soft but not mushy. When potatoes and turnips are done, work quickly. Drain and shake off excess water. Run vegetables through a food mill or potato ricer. Add butter while they are still hot. If you like, you can run the butter through the mill along with the vegetables. Add milk or cream and salt and pepper.

WHIPPED SWEET POTATOES

PREP TIME: 40 minutes

FEEDS: 4

3 pounds sweet potatoes

9 tablespoons butter

¾ cup maple syrup

Pinch hot chile powder

¾ teaspoon salt

Pinch pepper

Peel sweet potatoes and cut into 3-inch-thick pieces. Place in a pot of boiling salted water and cook until soft. Keep an eye on them because the sweet potatoes will quickly start to disintegrate when they are done. Process in a food mill with remaining ingredients.

 Be sure to use real maple syrup.

GRITS SPOON BREAD

PREP TIME: 1½ hours

FEEDS: 4

1 cup instant grits
½ tablespoon salt
1 tablespoon sugar
½ gallon milk
9 eggs
Butter to coat pan

 This is a really fun dish. I think of it as a southern soufflé.

In a saucepan mix together grits, salt, and sugar. Combine with milk and bring to a simmer. Cook for 5 minutes. Let cool. Grits mixture must cool down before proceeding to the next step.

Preheat oven to 325 degrees F. Separate eggs. Blend yolks with grits and whip egg whites to soft peaks. Fold whites into the grits mixture. Place the batter in a buttered shallow 9- x 12-inch pan. Bake for about 40 minutes, or until set. The spoon bread will rise up. Serve immediately, as you would a soufflé.

COLLARD GREENS

PREP TIME: 45 minutes

FEEDS: 4 to 6

1 ham hock
2 bunches collard greens
½ large onion in large dice
2 teaspoons minced garlic
¼ cup vegetable oil
2½ cups stock or water
2 dashes Tabasco
2 tablespoons apple cider
   vinegar
Salt to taste
Pepper to taste

In a stock pot, cover the ham hock with stock or water and simmer it for 45 minutes to 1 hour before starting to cook the collards. This will be the base for good potlikker. Remove the ham hock. When cool, dice the meat, removing and discarding skin, fat, and gristle. The ham bone can be re-used for cooking beans.

Cut collards across into 1½-inch strips. Discard thick part of the stem at the bottom. Soak in cold water to clean. Sauté diced onions and garlic in oil for 2 or 3 minutes. Add the collards, stock or water in which you cooked the ham hock, Tabasco, vinegar, and a little salt and pepper. Be careful with the salt, as the ham hock is already salty. Bring to a boil, then turn down to a simmer. Cook for about 30 to 45 minutes, until tender. The actual cooking time will depend on the collard greens; they should not be undercooked. The fibers that run through the greens should be cooked through and soft, not at all chewy. Taste for seasoning.

INDEX

Boldface indicates a photograph.

Achiote paste, with Pollo Pibil, 134, **135**
Aioli, Garlic, with Smoky Spanish Paprika, 123
Ancho Chiles
    in Mole Colorado, 149
    in Red Chile, 148
Andouille sausage
    in Gumbo Ya Ya, 119
    in Jambalaya, 118
    Smoked Turkey, Sweet Potato, and
        Andouille Hash, 62
Apples
    Apple Pie, **30**, 31
    Dixon Apple Salad with Poppy Seed
        Dressing, 98, **99**
Apricot-Blackberry Crisp, 41
Artichokes, Grilled, with Mustard-Dill
    Vinaigrette, **86**, 87
Asafetida, in Indian Shrimp Fritters, **76**, 77
Asian Salmon Marinade, with Asian
    Grilled Salmon with Fried Rice, 113
Avocado
    Avocado-Citrus Salad, **90**, 91
    Creamy Avocado Dressing with
        Roadhouse Veggie Chop, 97

Bacon
    Iceberg Salad with Bacon-
        Buttermilk Dressing, 93
    Pan-Fried Trout and Eggs with Bacon, 70
Bailey, Janet, 27
Banana, White Chocolate, Cream Pie, **30**, 33
Basil, Mustard-Basil Marinated Salmon, 114
BBQ, Roadhouse BBQ Chicken, 131
Beans
    Black Beans, 147
    Cowboy Beans, 148
    Refritos Negros, 147
Beef
    Carbonnade Flammade, 107
    Ethel's Jewish Pot Roast of Brisket
        with Gravy, 109
    Mexican Market–Style Steak (or
        Roadhouse Tampiquena), 111

Ropa Vieja, 102
Biscuits
    Biscuits, 59
    Red-Eye Gravy with Biscuits and Ham, 71
    Tomato Corn Biscuit Pie, **138**, 139
Black Beans, 147
Black Beans, in Refritos Negros, 147
Blackberries, Apricot-Blackberry Crisp, 41
Blood Oranges, in Avocado-Citrus Salad,
    90, 91
Blue Cornmeal Waffles, 52, **53**
Blueberries
    Blueberry Buckwheat Cakes, 50
    Blueberry or Cranberry Muffins, 58
    Blueberry Pie, 38, **39**
Bourbon
    Bourbon-Pecan Caramel Sauce, 22
    Cranberry-Bourbon Sauce with
        Polenta Cakes with Smoked Duck
        and Wild Rice, 79
Bread
    Biscuits, 59
    Blueberry or Cranberry Muffins, 58
    Bruschetta with Grouper in Crazy
        Water, **116**, 117
    Chicken 'n' Dumplings, 124
    Chocolate Bread Pudding, 22
    Chocolate French Toast, 54
    Cinnamon Rolls, **60**, 61
    Cinnamon-Sugar Muffins, **56**, 57
    Feather-Light Cornmeal Muffins, 54
    Goat Cheese Bruschetta, 92
    Grits Spoon Bread, 155
    Mocha Walnut Muffins, 59
    Pumpkin Muffins, 57
    Red-Eye Gravy with Biscuits and Ham, 71
    Tomato Corn Biscuit Pie, **138**, 139
Brisket, Ethel's Jewish Pot Roast of, with
    Gravy, 109
Brownies, Double Chocolate Espresso, 20, **21**
Bruschetta
    Goat Cheese Bruschetta, 92
    with Grouper in Crazy Water, **116**, 117
Buckwheat, Blueberry, Cakes, 50
Burrito, Breakfast, 64, **65**
Butter, Orange, 52

Buttermilk
    Buttermilk Pancakes, 50
    Iceberg Salad with Bacon-
        Buttermilk Dressing, 93
Butternut squash, Moroccan, Stew with
    Chickpeas and Spinach, 142, **143**
Butterscotch Pudding, in Lucky Pudding,
    24, **25**
Butterscotch Custard with Chocolate-
    Orange Sauce, 28

Cabbage
    Cabbage Rolls with Meat, 106
    Vegetarian Cabbage Rolls, 141
    Cabot cheese, in Tomato Corn
        Biscuit Pie, **138**, 139
Cakes
    Chesapeake Bay–Style Crab Cakes, 121, **122**
    Coffee Cake, 55
    Flourless Chocolate Cake, 45
    Fudgy Chocolate Layers, 42
    Polenta Cakes with Smoked Duck
        and Wild Rice, 79
Calabacitas, Frito Pie with, 140
Calamari, Fried, with Puttanesca Sauce, 120
Caramel, Bourbon-Pecan, Sauce, 22
Cascabel chiles, in Salsa Cascabel, 146
Chana besan, in Indian Shrimp Fritters, **76**, 77
Charmula, with Moroccan Butternut
    Squash Stew with Chickpeas and
    Spinach, 142, **143**
Cheese
    Goat Cheese Bruschetta, 92
    Queso Fundido with Mushrooms, 78
    Queso Fundido with Veggies, 78
Chicken
    Arroz con Pollo, 125
    Chicken 'n' Dumplings, 124
    Chicken Enchiladas Suiza, 127
    Chicken Piccata, 136
    Chicken Pot Pie, 128, **129**
    Fried Chicken, **132**, 133
    Jamaican Jerked Chicken, 130
    Pollo Pibil, 134, **135**
    Poulet Diablo, 130
    Roadhouse BBQ Chicken, 131

Chickpea Flour, in Indian Shrimp Fritters, **76**, 77
Chickpeas, Moroccan Butternut Squash Stew with, and Spinach, 142, **143**
Chocolate curls, how to make, 33
Chocolate
    Butterscotch Custard with Chocolate-Orange Sauce, 28
    Chocolate Bread Pudding, 22
    Chocolate Chunk Cookies, **26**, 27
    Chocolate French Toast, 54
    Chocolate Pudding, in Lucky Pudding, 24, **25**
    Double Chocolate Espresso Brownies, 20, **21**
    Flourless Chocolate Cake, 45
    Fudgy Chocolate Layers, 42
    in Mole Colorado, 149
    White Chocolate Banana Cream Pie, **30**, 33
Chorizo, in Migas, **66**, 67
Chowder, Chile Corn, 83
Chuck, in Carbonnade Flammade, 107
Cilantro Pesto, 152
Cinnamon
    Cinnamon Rolls, **60**, 61
    Cinnamon-Sugar Muffins, **56**, 57
Citrus
    Avocado-Citrus Salad, **90**, 91
    Citrus Vinaigrette with Avocado-Citrus Salad, **90**, 91
Cobbler, Peach, **40**, 41
Coconut
    Coconut Cream Pie, **30**, 32
    Coconut Pecan Icing, 43
Coffee
    Coffee Cake, 55
    Double Chocolate Espresso Brownies, 20, **21**
    Mocha Walnut Muffins, 59
Cookies, Chocolate Chunk, **26**, 27
Corn
    Chile Corn Chowder, 83
    Fried Green Tomato Salad with Sweet Corn Vinaigrette, 88, **89**
    Tomato Corn Biscuit Pie, **138**, 139
Corned Beef, in Red Flannel Hash, 62, **63**
Cornmeal, Feather-Light, Muffins, 54
Coulis, Tomato, 148
Couscous, with Moroccan Butternut Squash Stew with Chickpeas and Spinach, 142, **143**

Crab, Chesapeake Bay–Style, Cakes, 121, **122**
Cranberries
    Blueberry or Cranberry Muffins, 58
    Cranberry-Bourbon Sauce with Polenta Cakes with Smoked Duck and Wild Rice, 79
Crazy Water, Grouper in, **116**, 117
Custard, Butterscotch, with Chocolate-Orange Sauce, 28

Dill, Grilled Artichokes with Mustard-Dill Vinaigrette, **86**, 87
Dough, Pie, 29
Dressing
    Creamy Avocado Dressing with Roadhouse Veggie Chop, 97
    Dixon Apple Salad with Poppy Seed Dressing, 98, **99**
    Green Goddess Dressing with Roadhouse Hippie Salad, 94–95, **96**
    Iceberg Salad with Bacon-Buttermilk Dressing, 93
    Sesame Dressing with Roadhouse Hippie Salad, 94–95, **96**
Duck
    Polenta Cakes with Smoked Duck and Wild Rice, 79
    Smoked Duck Flautas with Mango Sauce, 74, **75**
Dumplings, Chicken 'n' Dumplings, 124

Eclairs, 44–45
Eggs
    Chile Rellenos Omelet, 68
    Green Eggs and Ham, 70
    Huevos Divorciados, 67
    Huevos En Brodo, 69
    Huevos Motulenos, 64
    Migas, **66**, 67
    Pan-Fried Trout and Eggs with Bacon, 70
Enchiladas
    Chicken Enchiladas Suiza, 127
    Vegetable Enchiladas, 137
    Espresso, Double Chocolate, Brownies, 20, **21**

Figs, Caramelized, with Prosciutto and Hazelnuts, 93

Flautas, Smoked Duck, with Mango Sauce, 74, **75**
French Toast, Chocolate, 54
Frito Pie with Calabacitas, 140
Fritters, Indian Shrimp, **76**, 77
Frosting
    Coconut Pecan Icing, 43
    Fudgy Frosting, 43
Fruits
    Apple Pie, **30**, 31
    Apricot-Blackberry Crisp, 41
    Avocado-Citrus Salad, **90**, 91
    Blueberry Buckwheat Cakes, 50
    Blueberry or Cranberry Muffins, 58
    Blueberry Pie, 38, **39**
    Butterscotch Custard with Chocolate-Orange Sauce, 28
    Caramelized Figs with Prosciutto and Hazelnuts, 93
    Cranberry-Bourbon Sauce with Polenta Cakes with Smoked Duck and Wild Rice, 79
    Dixon Apple Salad with Poppy Seed Dressing, 98, **99**
    Fried Green Tomato Salad with Sweet Corn Vinaigrette, 88, **89**
    Grilled Pork Chop with Plum Salsa, **104**, 105
    Lemon Meringue Pie, 34, **35**
    Lemon Poppy Seed Waffles, 51
    Mango Sauce, 150
    Orange Butter, 52
    Peach Cobbler, **40**, 41
    Saffron-Lemon Mayonnaise, 123
    Smoked Duck Flautas with Mango Sauce, 74, **75**
    Sopa de Lima, 82
    Strawberry-Lemon Ricotta Cakes, 48, **49**
    Strawberry-Rhubarb Pie, **30**, 36, 37
    Tomato Coulis, 148
    White Chocolate Banana Cream Pie, **30**, 33

Ganache, in Eclairs, 44–45
Garlic
    Garlic Aioli with Smoky Spanish Paprika, 123
    Yukon Gold Potatoes with Roasted Garlic, 153
Goat Cheese Bruschetta, 92

Granola, Roadhouse, 58
Gravy
    Country Gravy, 68
    Ethel's Jewish Pot Roast of Brisket
        with Gravy, 109
    Red-Eye Gravy with Biscuits and Ham, 71
Green Chile, 150
Green chiles
    in Breakfast Burrito, 64, **65**
    in Chile Rellenos Omelet, 68
    in Green Chile, 150
    in Green Eggs and Ham, 70
Greens, Collard, 155
Grits
    Grits Spoon Bread, 155
    Shrimp and Grits, 81
Grouper in Crazy Water, **116**, 117
Gumbo Ya Ya, 119

Häagen Dazs, 20
Haetter, Mae, 55
Halibut with Posole in Southwestern
    Roasted Vegetable Sauce, 115
Ham
    Green Eggs and Ham, 70
    Red-Eye Gravy with Biscuits and Ham, 71
Harissa, with Moroccan Butternut Squash
    Stew with Chickpeas and Spinach, 142, **143**
Hash
    Red Flannel Hash, 62, **63**
    Smoked Turkey, Sweet Potato, and
        Andouille Hash, 62
Hazelnuts, Caramelized Figs with
    Prosciutto and, 93
Herb-Crusted Stuffed Pork Chops, 103
Higgins, Caroline, 28

Iceberg lettuce, Iceberg Salad with Bacon-
    Buttermilk Dressing, 93
Icing, Coconut Pecan, 43
Indian Shrimp Fritters, **76**, 77

Jamaican Jerked Chicken, 130
Jambalaya, 118

Lamb Fajitas, 110
Lemon
    Lemon Meringue Pie, 34, **35**

Lemon Poppy Seed Waffles, 51
    Saffron-Lemon Mayonnaise, 123
    Strawberry-Lemon Ricotta Cakes, 48, **49**
Limes, Sopa de Lima, 82

Mango
    Mango Sauce, 150
    Smoked Duck Flautas with Mango
        Sauce, 74, **75**
Marinara, with Meatballs, 112
Mayonnaise
    Basic Mayonnaise, 123
    Saffron-Lemon Mayonnaise, 123
Meat Loaf, Roadhouse Turkey, 126
Meatballs, 112
Meringue
    how to make, 35
    Lemon Meringue Pie, 34, **35**
Mesclun, in Grilled Artichokes with
    Mustard-Dill Vinaigrette, **86**, 87
Mexican chocolate, in Mole Colorado, 149
Mexican chorizo
    in Queso Fundido with Mushrooms, 78
    in Queso Fundido with Veggies, 78
Mocha Walnut Muffins, 59
Muffins
    Blueberry or Cranberry Muffins, 58
    Cinnamon-Sugar Muffins, **56**, 57
    Feather-Light Cornmeal Muffins, 54
    Mocha Walnut Muffins, 59
    Pumpkin Muffins, 57
Mushrooms
    Magic Mushroom Powder in
        Roadhouse Hippie Salad, 94–95, **96**
    Queso Fundido with Mushrooms, 78
    Trout with Mushroom, Pine Nut,
        and Sage Stuffing, 114
Mustard
    Grilled Artichokes with Mustard-
        Dill Vinaigrette, **86**, 87
    Mustard-Basil Marinated Salmon, 114

Nakamura, Joel, 24

Oaxaqueno cheese, in Mexican Market–
    Style Steak (or Roadhouse Tampiquena),
    111
Omelet, Chile Rellenos, 68

Onions
    Pickled Red Onion, 151
    Vidalia Onion Rings in Roadhouse
        Hippie Salad, 94–95, **96**
Oranges
    Butterscotch Custard with Orange
        Custard Sauce, 28
    Orange Butter, 52

Pancakes
    Blueberry Buckwheat Cakes, 50
    Buttermilk Pancakes, 50
    how to make, 48
    Strawberry-Lemon Ricotta Cakes,
        48, **49**
    Wild Rice Pancakes, 152
Panela cheese, in Huevos En Brodo, 69
Panna Cotta, Vanilla, 27
Paprika, Garlic Aioli with Smoky Spanish,
    123
Pasilla negros
    in Red Chile, 148
    in Vegetable Enchiladas, 137
Peach Cobbler, **40**, 41
Pecans
    Bourbon-Pecan Caramel Sauce, 22
    Brent's Famous Candied Pecans, 150
    Coconut Pecan Icing, 43
    Pecan Pie, **30**, 31
Pecorino cheese
    in Meatballs, 112
    in Queso Fundido with Veggies, 78
    in Roadhouse Turkey Meat Loaf, 126
Pesto, Cilantro, 152
Pibil Marinade, with Pollo Pibil, 134, **135**
Piccata Sauce, with Chicken Piccata, 136
Piccata, Chicken, 136
Pie pumpkins, how to roast, 37
Pie shell, how to precook, 32
Pies
    Apple Pie, **30**, 31
    Blueberry Pie, 38, **39**
    Chicken Pot Pie, 128, **129**
    Coconut Cream Pie, **30**, 32
    Frito Pie with Calabacitas, 140
    Lemon Meringue Pie, 34, **35**
    Pecan Pie, **30**, 31
    Pie Dough, 29

Pumpkin Pie, 37
Strawberry-Rhubarb Pie, **30**, **36**, 37
Tomato Corn Biscuit Pie, **138**, 139
White Chocolate Banana Cream
    Pie, **30**, 33
Pine Nuts, Trout with Mushroom, and Sage
    Stuffing, 114
Pineapples, in Tropical Pico do Gallo, 151
Pinto Beans, in Cowboy Beans, 148
Plantains, with Huevos Motulenos, 64
Plum, Grilled Pork Chop with, Salsa, **104**,
    105
Poblano chiles
    in Chile Corn Chowder, 83
    in Cilantro Pesto, 152
    in Cowboy Beans, 148
    in Huevos En Brodo, 69
    in Mexican Market–Style Steak (or
        Roadhouse Tampiquena), 111
    in Queso Fundido with Mushrooms, 78
    in Queso Fundido with Veggies, 78
    in Roadhouse Veggie Chop, 97
    in Smoked Turkey, Sweet Potato, and
        Andouille Hash, 62
    in Vegetable Enchiladas, 137
    Polenta Cakes with Smoked Duck
        and Wild Rice, 79
Poppy Seeds
    Dixon Apple Salad with Poppy Seed
        Dressing, 98, **99**
    Lemon Poppy Seed Waffles, 51
Pork
    Grilled Pork Chop with Plum Salsa, **104**, 105
    Herb-Crusted Stuffed Pork Chops, 103
    Roadhouse-Style Pulled Pork, 110
    Smothered Country-Style Pork Ribs, 108
Posole, Halibut with, in Southwestern
    Roasted Vegetable Sauce, 115
Pot Roast, Ethel's Jewish, of Brisket with
    Gravy, 109
Potatoes
    Mashed Potatoes, 153
    Potato Salad, 95
    Potato-Turnip Puree, 154
    Red Flannel Hash, 62, **63**
    Smoked Turkey, Sweet Potato, and
        Andouille Hash, 62
    Whipped Sweet Potatoes, 154

Yukon Gold Potatoes with Roasted
    Garlic, 153
Prosciutto, Caramelized Figs with, and
    Hazelnuts, 93
Pudding
    Chocolate Bread Pudding, 22
    Lucky Pudding, 24, **25**
Pumpkin
    Pumpkin Muffins, 57
    Pumpkin Pie, 37
    Pumpkin Waffles, 52
Puree, Potato-Turnip, 154
Puttanesca, Fried Calamari with, Sauce, 120

Queso Oaxaquena, in Huevos En Brodo, 69

Rajas, in Lamb Fajitas, 110
Red Chile, 148
    Red chiles, in Breakfast Burrito, 64, **65**
Red Onion, Pickled, 151
Red Sauce, with Vegetable Enchiladas, 137
Rhubarb, Strawberry-Rhubarb Pie, **30**, **36**, 37
Ribs, Smothered Country-Style Pork, 108
Rice
    Arroz con Pollo, 125
    Asian Grilled Salmon with Fried Rice, 113
    Polenta Cakes with Smoked Duck
        and Wild Rice, 79
    Wild Rice Pancakes, 152
    Ricotta, Strawberry-Lemon, Cakes, 48, **49**
Rolls
    Cabbage Rolls with Meat, 106
    Cinnamon Rolls, **60**, 61
    Vegetarian Cabbage Rolls, 141

Saffron-Lemon Mayonnaise, 123
Sage, Trout with Mushroom, Pine Nut,
    and, Stuffing, 114
Salmon
    Asian Grilled Salmon with Fried
        Rice, 113
    Mustard-Basil Marinated Salmon, 114
Salsa
    Grilled Pork Chop with Plum Salsa, **104**, 105
    Habanero Salsa, 151
    Salsa Cascabel, 146
    Suiza, 146
    Tomatillo Salsa, 146

Tropical Pico do Gallo, 151
Sambal sauce, in Sesame Dressing with
    Roadhouse Hippie Salad, 94–95, **96**
Sauces
    Basic Mayonnaise, 123
    Bourbon-Pecan Caramel Sauce, 22
    Butterscotch Custard with Orange
        Custard Sauce, 28
    Chicken Enchiladas Suiza, 127
    Cilantro Pesto, 152
    Cranberry-Bourbon Sauce with
        Polenta Cakes with Smoked Duck
        and Wild Rice, 79
    Fried Calamari with Puttanesca Sauce, 120
    Garlic Aioli with Smoky Spanish
        Paprika, 123
    Grouper in Crazy Water, **116**, 117
    Halibut with Posole in Southwestern
        Roasted Vegetable Sauce, 115
    Mango Sauce, 150
    Mole Colorado, 149
    Piccata Sauce with Chicken Piccata, 136
    Red Sauce with Vegetable Enchiladas, 137
    Saffron-Lemon Mayonnaise, 123
    Smoked Duck Flautas with Mango
        Sauce, 74, **75**
    Tartar Sauce, 123
    Texas BBQ Sauce with Roadhouse
        BBQ Chicken, 131
Sausage
    Andouille sausage in Gumbo Ya Ya, 119
    Andouille sausage in Jambalaya, 118
    Smoked Turkey, Sweet Potato, and
        Andouille Hash, 62
Scotch bonnets, in Jamaican Jerked
    Chicken, 130
Seafood
    Asian Grilled Salmon with Fried Rice, 113
    Bayou-Spiced Shrimp, 80
    Chesapeake Bay–Style Crab Cakes, 121, **122**
    Fried Calamari with Puttanesca Sauce, 120
    Grouper in Crazy Water, **116**, 117
    Gumbo Ya Ya, 119
    Halibut with Posole in Southwestern
        Roasted Vegetable Sauce, 115
    Indian Shrimp Fritters, **76**, 77
    Jambalaya, 118
    Mustard-Basil Marinated Salmon, 114

Pan-Fried Trout and Eggs with Bacon, 70
Shrimp and Grits, 81
Trout with Mushroom, Pine Nut,
    and Sage Stuffing, 114
Sesame Dressing with Roadhouse Hippie
    Salad, 94–95, **96**
Sherry, Wilted Spinach Salad with Warm,
    Vinaigrette, 92
Shrimp
    Bayou-Spiced Shrimp, 80
    Indian Shrimp Fritters, **76**, 77
    Shrimp and Grits, 81
    Smoky Spanish Paprika, Garlic Aioli
        with, 123
Soups
    Chile Corn Chowder, 83
    Moroccan Butternut Squash Stew with
        Chickpeas and Spinach, 142, **143**
    Mulligatawny, 82
    Sopa de Lima, 82
Spinach
    Moroccan Butternut Squash Stew
        with Chickpeas and Spinach,
        142, **143**
    Wilted Spinach Salad with Warm
        Sherry Vinaigrette, 92
Squash
    Moroccan Butternut Squash Stew
        with Chickpeas and Spinach,
        142, **143**
    Stuffed Squash Blossoms, 80
Steak
    Mexican Market–Style Steak (or
        Roadhouse Tampiquena), 111
    Ropa Vieja, 102
    Stew, Moroccan Butternut Squash, with
        Chickpeas and Spinach, 142, **143**
Strawberries
    Strawberry-Lemon Ricotta Cakes, 48, **49**
    Strawberry-Rhubarb Pie, **30**, **36**, 37
Stuffing, Trout with Mushroom, Pine Nut,
    and Sage, 114
Suiza, Chicken Enchiladas, 127
Sweet Corn, Fried Green Tomato Salad
    with, Vinaigrette, 88, **89**

Tahini, in Sesame Dressing with Roadhouse
    Hippie Salad, 94–95, **96**

Tamatar Chutney, with Indian Shrimp
    Fritters, **76**, 77
Tartar Sauce, 123
Texas BBQ Sauce, with Roadhouse BBQ
    Chicken, 131
Tomatillo Salsa, 146
Tomatoes
    Fried Green Tomato Salad with
        Sweet Corn Vinaigrette, 88, **89**
    Tomato Corn Biscuit Pie, **138**, 139
    Tomato Coulis, 148
Topping, Crisp, 41
Trout
    Pan-Fried Trout and Eggs with Bacon, 70
    Trout with Mushroom, Pine Nut,
        and Sage Stuffing, 114
Turkey
    Roadhouse Turkey Meat Loaf, 126
    Smoked Turkey, Sweet Potato, and
        Andouille Hash, 62
Turnips, Potato-Turnip Puree, 154

Vanilla Panna Cotta, 27
Vegetables
    Avocado-Citrus Salad, **90**, 91
    Cabbage Rolls with Meat, 106
    Caramelized Figs with Prosciutto
        and Hazelnuts, 93
    Chile Corn Chowder, 83
    Collard Greens, 155
    Dixon Apple Salad with Poppy Seed
        Dressing, 98, **99**
    Fried Green Tomato Salad with
        Sweet Corn Vinaigrette, 88, **89**
    Frito Pie with Calabacitas, 140
    Grilled Artichokes with Mustard-
        Dill Vinaigrette, **86**, 87
    Halibut with Posole in Southwestern
        Roasted Vegetable Sauce, 115
    Iceberg Salad with Bacon-
        Buttermilk Dressing, 93
    Mashed Potatoes, 153
    Moroccan Butternut Squash Stew with
        Chickpeas and Spinach, 142, **143**
    Pickled Red Onion, 151
    Potato Salad, 95
    Potato-Turnip Puree, 154
    Pumpkin Muffins, 57

Pumpkin Pie, 37
Pumpkin Waffles, 52
Roadhouse Hippie Salad, 94–95, **96**
Roadhouse Veggie Chop, 97
Stuffed Squash Blossoms, 80
Tomato Corn Biscuit Pie, **138**, 139
Trout with Mushroom, Pine Nut,
    and Sage Stuffing, 114
Vegetable Enchiladas, 137
Vegetarian Cabbage Rolls, 141

Whipped Sweet Potatoes, 154
Wilted Spinach Salad with Warm Sherry
    Vinaigrette, 92

Yukon Gold Potatoes with Roasted Garlic,
    153
Vidalia Onion Rings in Roadhouse Hippie
    Salad, 94–95, **96**
Vinaigrettes
    Citrus Vinaigrette with Avocado-
        Citrus Salad, **90**, 91
    Fried Green Tomato Salad with
        Sweet Corn Vinaigrette, 88, **89**
    Grilled Artichokes with Mustard-Dill
        Vinaigrette, **86**, 87
    Wilted Spinach Salad with Warm
        Sherry Vinaigrette, 92

Waffles
    Blue Cornmeal Waffles, 52, **53**
    how to make, 51
    Lemon Poppy Seed Waffles, 51
    Pumpkin Waffles, 52
Walnut, Mocha, Muffins, 59
White Chocolate Banana Cream Pie, **30**, 33

Yukon Gold Potatoes with Roasted Garlic,
    153